601 WOODSHOP TIPS & TRICKS

GRAHAM McCULLOCH

POPULAR WOODWORKING BOOKS
CINCINNATI, OHIO
www.popularwoodworking.com

READ THIS IMPORTANT SAFETY NOTICE

To prevent accidents, keep safety in mind while you work. Use the safety guards installed on power equipment; they are for your protection.

When working on power equipment, keep fingers away from saw blades, wear safety goggles to prevent injuries from flying wood chips and sawdust, wear hearing protection and consider installing a dust vacuum to reduce the amount of airborne sawdust in your woodshop.

Don't wear loose clothing, such as neckties or shirts with loose sleeves, or jewelry, such as rings, necklaces or bracelets, when working on power equipment. Tie back long hair to prevent it from getting caught in your equipment.

People who are sensitive to certain chemicals should check the chemical content of any product before using it.

Due to the variability of local conditions, construction materials, skill levels, etc., neither the author nor Popular Woodworking Books assumes any responsibility for any accidents, injuries, damages or other losses incurred resulting from the material presented in this book.

The authors and editors who compiled this book have tried to make the contents as accurate and correct as possible. Plans, illustrations, photographs and text have been carefully checked. All instructions, plans and projects should be carefully read, studied and understood before beginning construction.

Prices listed for supplies and equipment were current at the time of publication and are subject to change.

METRIC CONVERSION CHART

to convert	to	multiply by
Inches	Centimeters	2.54
Centimeters	Inches	0.4
Feet	Centimeters	30.5
Centimeters	Feet	0.03
Yards	Meters	0.9
Meters	Yards	1.1

601 WOODSHOP TIPS & TRICKS. Copyright © 2010 by Graham McCulloch. Printed and bound in China. All rights reserved. No part of this book may be reproduced in any form or by any electronic or mechanical means including information storage and retrieval systems without permission in writing from the publisher, except by a reviewer, who may quote brief passages in a review. Published by Popular Woodworking Books, an imprint of F+W Media, Inc., 4700 East Galbraith Road, Cincinnati, Ohio, 45236. First edition.

Distributed in Canada by Fraser Direct
100 Armstrong Avenue
Georgetown, Ontario L7G 5S4
Canada

Distributed in the U.K. and Europe by David & Charles
Brunel House
Newton Abbot
Devon TQ12 4PU
England
Tel: (+44) 1626 323200
Fax: (+44) 1626 323319
E-mail: postmaster@davidandcharles.co.uk

Distributed in Australia by Capricorn Link
P.O. Box 704
Windsor, NSW 2756
Australia

Visit our Website at www.popularwoodworking.com.

Other fine Popular Woodworking Books are available from your local bookstore or direct from the publisher.

14   13   12   11   10   5   4   3   2   1

Library of Congress Cataloging-in-Publication Data

McCulloch, Graham.
   601 woodshop tips & tricks / Graham McCulloch. -- 1st ed.
      p. cm.
   ISBN 978-1-4403-0169-8 (pbk. : alk. paper)
   1. Woodwork. 2. Woodworking tools. 3. Workshops--Equipment and supplies. I. Title. II. Title: Six hundred and one woodshop tips & tricks.
   TT185.M21254 2010
   684'.08--dc22
                                        2009050917

ACQUISITIONS EDITOR: David Thiel
SENIOR EDITOR: Jim Stack
COVER DESIGNER: Doug Mayfield
INTERIOR DESIGNER: Brian Roeth
PRODUCTION COORDINATOR: Mark Griffin
PHOTOGRAPHER: Graham McCulloch
ILLUSTRATOR: Dylan Edwards and Hayes Shanesy

ABOUT THE AUTHOR

 Graham McCulloch has been a woodworker for close to 65 years having just turned 75 (at this writing). With this one, Graham now has five woodworking books under his belt the last of which is *The Woodworker's Illustrated Encyclopedia*.

Graham found his love for making sawdust at the age of 10 in grade school in Montreal. Back then it was called sloyd and he quickly developed a love for the craft. Later, the author became an architectural designer creating a vast number of furniture pieces and cabinetry in Montreal.

Nova Scotia always had a special place in his heart and after many visits 'Down Home' to visit relatives; Graham made the move in 1979. Settling in Halifax he opened a trade show exhibit design and construction business.

Graham continued the business for many years until he decided to retire. He was very successful in all of his endeavors except for the last one. As a retiree, Graham is an absolute failure. Designing and furniture building is his passion and it is difficult to give it up. Graham is a Director for the Atlantic Woodworker's Association and a member of the Nova Scotia Federation of Anglers and Hunters and is an avid photographer. He now lives with his wife in a Halifax suburb.

Graham continues to write about woodworking in a bi-weekly column on his website at http://www.shortcuts.ns.ca and for the *Canadian Woodworking and Home Improvement* magazine as well as *The Contractor's Desk Magazine*.

DEDICATION

As always, this book is dedicated to Gwen, my wife, my love.

And, to my many friends here in Halifax, Nova Scotia that include Bryan and Jackie, Fred and Linda, Rex and Bev, Lynn and Kenny, Rob, Ken, Carter, John and Judy, Tony and Sally, Ross, Ron and more whose names escape me right now.

Special thanks go out to Wilf (Woody) Woods for his assistance with the many photographs seen in the book. We spent many hours in my shop setting up the shots, doing the lighting and then the final cropping.

Black & Decker Canada also deserves my gratitude; B&D is the parent company of DeWalt, Delta and Porter-Cable. Black & Decker supplied all of the power tools that are illustrated in the book.

WOODSHOP TIPS FOR:

INTRODUCTION

The Random House Dictionary definition:
Shortcuts *1) A shorter or quicker way or route.
2) Any method that cuts down time and energy.*

Graham McCulloch's definition:
Shortcuts *Easier and more efficient ways to achieve excellent results.*
Jig *A shop-made device designed to assist in the making of accurate repetitive work.*

Having been a woodworker both as an amateur and a professional for over 60 years, I have learned and/or developed a long list of shortcuts that have helped me and my fellow woodworkers save time, material and effort to achieve our final results.

Before the days of the computer I used to write or type my newly learned or discovered shortcuts on 3½" × 5" recipe cards and file them in a steel file box on my workbench. The cards were filed alphabetically according to the tool that they were used for. Later, with the introduction of the home computer, these cards were then transcribed onto floppy discs. It was then that I realized that perhaps there are other woodworkers out there that would like to share in my collection.

Shortcuts generally are real time savers especially for repetitive work situations. It may take a little more time to make a jig initially but once made, the jig will save hours upon hours of time while assuring the woodworker of more precision in the duplication of his/her workpieces.

This book then is a culmination of over 600 shortcuts amassed over the years and presented grouped by category for easy reference. The shop tips are listed in reference to either the woodworking tool itself, (e.g. Table Saw) an accessory to the tool (e.g. Dado Blade) or a woodworking process (e.g. Wood Finishing) to make the use of this book easier.

My aim in writing this book is not to show you how to build that entertainment center, my aim is to show you how to build it better and easier and certainly with less waste. Keep this book on your workbench or at least, in your workshop. You will be glad you did.

Since the late 1990s, *ShortCuts* has been an extremely popular website. We publish a bi-weekly column with woodworking and do-it-yourself topics and it brings the viewer right up to date with new woodworking methods and tools. You can see *ShortCuts* at http://www.shortcuts.ns.ca and if you wish, get a free subscription.

SHOP PLANNING

Any woodshop with the basic woodworking machinery and tools that works for you is really all that is required. After all, it will be you that will be spending time in it. However, having said that, there are some basic ideas that will make your time in that shop more pleasurable and equally important, more efficient.

The first step is to decide where to put your new shop and to draw up a plan. You can simply take pencil to paper (grid paper works best) or use any of the available home design (CAD) programs either online or through a software retailer.

There are books available showing how to set up your garage woodshop, most notably David Thiel's book titled *Woodshop Lust*. Woodworkers love to visit other woodworker's shops to "borrow" ideas for their own.

For the home woodworkers they usually have three location choices: The basement, the garage or an out-building. My experience has shown that most opt for the basement or the garage. Choosing the basement option means that it must have a convenient way to bring in raw materials and to remove the finished workpieces. You do not want to become the brunt of an urban myth by building an oversized project like a boat or large entertainment center that can't be removed from your shop.

The illustration below is the layout for my shop. The shop is in our basement uses half of the total foundation as the house is a back split design with four levels. The other half of the basement is unexcavated and is a crawl space.

There are two ways for materials and finished workpieces to enter and exit. The window on the north wall is custom built. The two panels open inwards and are at ground level outside. Or, we can carry material through the house and down

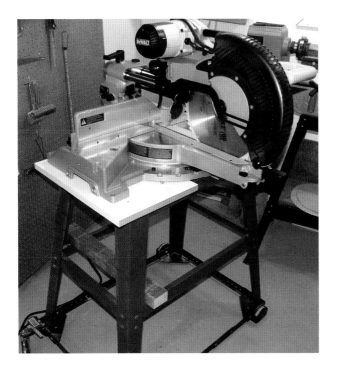

Mobile bases, like the one shown with my miter saw, make a shop adjustable, and because tools can be stored out of the way, smaller shops are more efficient. The flip-top planer, shown below, gives you two tools in a single footprint.

the stairs. This is not ideal but it works for us. The small window in the southwest wall is actually an exhaust fan and there is an air cleaner in the shop as well. This is, by normal standards, a small shop and I have made it considerably more efficient by placing my router table, miter saw, sander and thickness planer on casters. They can be easily moved into position as required without any effort whatsoever.

One other space saving solution is a mobile flip-top tool stand. These contain two tools, like a thickness planer and perhaps a spindle sander or any other two bench-top tools. Plans for this can be found on the internet. The photo shown is for example only.

the single car garage

The single car garage option of course relegates the family car to driveway parking.

I have included two very basic floor plans for garage woodshops, one for a single car garage and the other for a double car garage. The latter being somewhat better and, it allows the family vehicle to occupy one bay. For northern climates this would be the better choice.

Before designing your shop, take a look at some of the commercial cabinetmaker's shops. Most will be more than happy to show you around. You will then find that the most efficient woodshops are those built to work in an inverted U-shaped configuration. This allows the raw material to be brought into the shop and then proceed in a natural progression of processing.

Professional shops will have their lumber racks close to the freight door for convenience.

Rough lumber is considerably less expensive than finished wood, so owning a thickness planer will pay for itself over time. Installing one on a mobile base and positioning it near the garage door would make sense. The table saw (or radial arm saw) should be centrally placed, being certain that there is at least eight feet of clear space in front of and behind the saw to allow for the ripping of sheet material.

PHOTO COURTESY OF DAVID COLE

Sawdust is a major factor that must be addressed in any woodshop but even more so in a home shop. You certainly do not want sawdust to penetrate the living space. In addition to installing an exhaust fan and an air cleaner, an efficient dust collection system should be considered. Sealing all seams and joints leading to the living space will be necessary as well.

Forced-air heating and air conditioning present additional problems for the home woodshop owner to consider. In a basement shop where there may be an air return the woodworker should install a separate filter to prevent sawdust from getting into the plenum of the furnace/air conditioner. The door to the living space should be an exterior type metal door with a magnetic jamb seal and a tight seal (sweep) at the sill. The woodworker should be sure that the filter is checked and/or changed regularly.

Before moving any equipment into the garage shop area, the cement floor should be sealed and painted with a high quality product. Epoxy would be best. The walls should be painted as well, as a good, high quality glossy paint finish will help to keep the sawdust from adhering to them.

the two car garage

The two car garage is perhaps the best situation (short of an out building) for a home woodshop. You will have some preparatory work to do before you can make full use of it however. For example, you will have to build a floor-to-ceiling dividing wall to split the two spaces. Care should be taken here as well to seal the wall tightly. A pocket door between the two areas will save space. The door to the home interior should be a metal clad door with a magnetic seal. You will see in the illustration at right that space for lumber has been provided in the vehicle area that shouldn't interfere with parking the car.

I purposely placed the shop area on the left or the far side of the garage to help with the dissipation of sawdust and noise. Like all woodshops, an efficient exhaust fan should be used and an air-filtering system and dust collection should be considered. Of course during the summer months you will invariably have both garage doors open and that in itself will help to alleviate the dust problems.

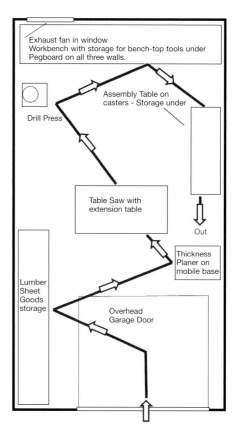

Single Car Garage Woodshop

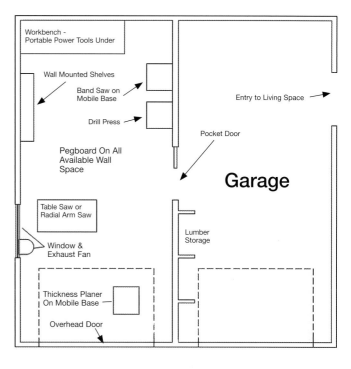

Two-Car Garage Woodshop

floors and ceilings

Almost any standard type of flooring will work for a woodshop floor as long as it is dry and solid. The shop floor must be able to support some heavy woodworking tools without flexing. A solid ¾"- thick plywood floor screwed on 16" centers will work, as will a poured concrete floor. Both types should be primed and painted to a smooth finish. This will make it easier to remove sawdust and to basically keep the floor clean. Light-colored epoxy-type paints will last a long time.

Your shop should have a fully finished ceiling for a number of reasons; noise and sawdust are just two of them. There are a number of material choices to be used here as well but certainly the most economical is plasterboard. Prime and paint the ceiling with a light color for light reflection.

To keep the noise somewhat muted in the adjacent living space, I suggest the use of rockwool batts rather than fiberglass. Air ducts should have flapper-type gates installed to prevent sawdust from entering them and to reduce the noise factor. Air returns, if any, should have filters installed in them.

lighting

Proper ambient and task lighting is imperative in a woodshop. Shadows created by poor lighting can really make a difference in measuring accuracy. Fluorescent 2×4 fixtures with daylight or cool-white tubes in them are good for ambient, shadow-free lighting.

Task lighting is very important for the woodworker. Pencil lines can be difficult to see without the proper lighting and ceiling hung fixtures will make measurements and reference lines

and the like easier to read. A task light should be placed above each stationary power tool and of course, over your workbench.

I have found that simple drapery track can be used to hang these fixtures and it makes it easy to shift them for better visibility. This is especially true with tools on mobile bases. The new compact fluorescent lights (CFL's) are excellent as well as being real money savers. I have installed three, 42-watt (the equivalent of 150 watts) cool-white CFL's over my workbench and they give me perfect light.

There is nothing like a low-angle light shining across the top of your workpiece to highlight any sanding or finishing flaws. I use a DeWalt lightweight job-site fluorescent for this because it is compact and easily stored.

Having separate switches for each of these individual lights is convenient and it is also nice to have them wired into a separate circuit-breaker box. By

doing this your shop lights can all be turned on or off with the flick of a couple of panel breakers. In fact, it is a good idea to have your entire woodshop wired into that same circuit-breaker box. This will allow you to power down all of your stationary power tools as well.

Should your spouse decide to do the vacuuming at the same time that you turn on your table saw, you can expect a circuit breaker to trip off. This is an additional benefit of having dedicated circuits for your stationary shop tools. Some tools will draw enough power to warrant a dedicated circuit for them. Your tool's manual will provide this information for you.

electrical outlets

Most woodshops that I have been in have a plethora of electrical outlets in every conceivable empty space. This is true where the shop uses tools on mobile bases. On one particular workbench, where I keep my benchtop tools, I have a long power bar. I try to make use of six- and eight-outlet power bars throughout the shop. The added bonus is that they all have built-in circuit breakers. And, they are all equipped with on/off switches.

Some shops have electrical power outlets hanging from the ceiling for further convenience. These can be hung closer to the floor with bungee cords attached. When not in use they will be out of the way. Should you want to install wall outlets it is best to install them 3'6" above the floor and a minimum of five feet apart.

There are some power outlets that you will want to keep "live" when shutting down for the night. These are the ones that you plug your cordless-tool battery chargers into.

clean air

You don't want to be breathing in sawdust all day, nor do you want that sawdust to enter your living space, so the best way to prevent this is to nip it in the bud.

I have a small window in my shop in which I have installed a pretty strong shop-built exhaust fan. This clears the air in the shop every 20 minutes or so and in the summertime helps to cool the air as well. A small basement or garage shop may not be conducive to a fixed-pipe dust collection system. I have my two-stage collector on wheels with a 6' length of 4" flexible hose that I simply attach to the tool that I will be using. I have a remote on/off switch that makes it more convenient.

My stationary tools are equipped with dust ports, so it is a simple and quick connection process. There are a number of attachments that are available for this type of system. A floor sweep is similar in shape to a dust pan and this can be placed or fixed to your workbench. When you are using your sander with the sweep connected it will suck up the sawdust at the source.

The dust collector is connected to a power supply that is remotely controlled. The remote switch is kept in my shop apron so I can turn on the collector

wherever I am in the shop. I don't have to go to the machine to switch it on or off.

My shop also has a sawdust and air filtration unit that is suspended from the ceiling joists. I have it hung with isolation straps that reduce the noise in the living space. There are some that claim that all these do is disturb settled dust but I have not found this to be true. My wife has allergies and there doesn't seem to be any sawdust entering the house from the shop.

One more reason to get rid of most of the sawdust is finishing. Should you be doing any finishing within your shop space you will really appreciate that it is nearly dust-free.

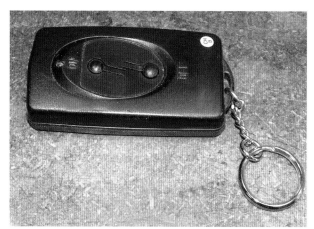

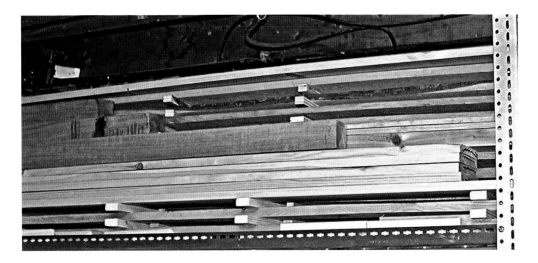

lumber storage

One of the biggest problems with a small home workshop is the storage of lumber and sheet goods, such as plywood and paneling. The storage should be close to the main door of the shop. You will find that this is most convenient, especially when unloading it and when starting a project. If your stationary tools are laid out as suggested, the lumber will be right at the beginning stage of your project.

Plywood and other sheet goods should be stored on their long edges and kept vertical. Cantilevered supports can then be mounted on the wall above and should be spaced every 16". Lumber can be very heavy, so there should be as much support as possible.

Lumber should be stored flat and, as long as it is dry, may be normally stacked. If the wood has a moisture content between 10 and 25 percent, the boards should be stickered. This is done to allow air to circulate through the boards to hasten the drying process. Stickers are simply strips of ¾" × 2" wood that are placed between the boards at 24" intervals. The stickers should all be in a vertical alignment in the stack.

Lumber that is still "wet" or "green" should not be brought into the workshop. Find a sheltered area outside, sticker the boards, and let them dry outside. Normally it will take one year per inch of thickness to bring the wood down to a 15 percent moisture content level. A workable moisture content for say, interior furniture work, should be 7 to 8 percent.

Wood is in a constant state of movement due to the moisture it expels or absorbs because of changes in its environment. Therefore, buy lumber for a furniture project several weeks in advance of the actual construction to allow it to acclimatize in your shop environment; this is especially true if your lumber supplier keeps their materials in an outside yard.

tool storage

There are many ways to store hand tools, and believe me when I say that you want to choose the most flexible method for the way you work. Whether you are starting your hobby workshop early in life or as a way of keeping busy in later years, you will accumulate more hand tools. The most important thing about tool storage is knowing where that specific tool is when you need it.

You may choose one or more ways such as a toolbox, metal tool cabinet, shelves, a home-built cabinet or pegboards.

The best way I have found of storing tools is through the use of a home-built tool cabinet and plenty of pegboard walls. Pegboard is a great way to cover up concrete foundation walls, but there should be a vapor barrier placed on the interior foundation walls first. This will minimize rust-creating moisture in the shop. Pegboard should be installed before you position your stationary tools.

telephone

If having a telephone in your workshop is important, one of the most effective additions to it is known as a Shop Flasher and is available at woodworking tool shops. The Shop Flasher has a microphone that attaches to your existing phone. When the phone rings, the Flasher amplifies it and activates a strobe light to get your attention.

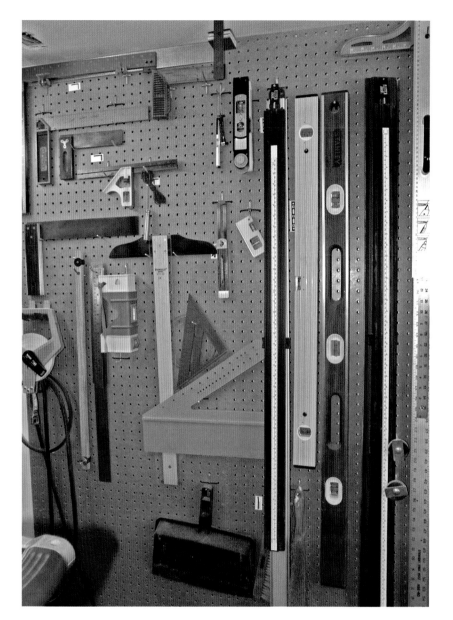

shop safety

In a millisecond you can lose a finger, eye or hand in a workshop. Sadly, I have seen it done. In each case it was through the negligence of the woodworker. The main causes of workshop injury are lack of attention and haste. Do not rush that job and pay very close attention to what you are doing. Follow these instructions:

Do not go into your workshop or operate power tools while under the influence of drugs (prescription or not) or alcohol.

Know and fully understand the operation of the tools that you are using (this includes familiarity with the owner's manual) and make sure that all of the tool's safety devices are working and in place.

Keep one or two fire extinguishers in convenient locations in your shop and make sure that they are maintained and charged regularly.

Avoid distractions while working with power tools. Even a slight distraction can be extremely dangerous. In the split second that your eyes leave the work, a disaster could occur. In a home workshop, members of your family should be aware of the dangers of entering the shop when tools are operating. A simple sign saying DO NOT ENTER IF TOOLS ARE RUNNING on the entry door will help as a reminder.

Wear the correct safety equipment, glasses or goggles, dust mask and hearing protection. Remember that some wood species may be highly toxic and could affect the respiratory system, eyes and/or skin. Some of the subject matter in the following chapter addresses safety concerns.

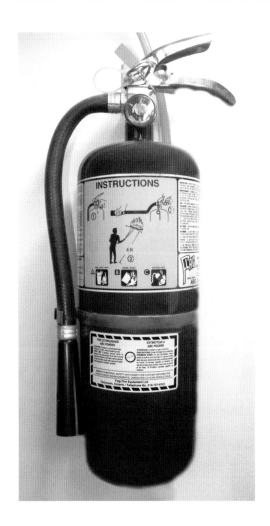

children in the shop

If there are children around, take special precautions. Young children are a curious lot. They love to experiment and play and do not realize that a sharp chisel or saw blade will quickly remove a finger or worse. Keep your workshop locked when not working there. Disconnect all of your stationary power tools; remove and hide the safety switch that most are equipped with. Having your shop on a separate circuit-breaker panel that can be locked is another deterrent. Portable power tools are easy to plug in and all children seem to learn this very quickly. A simple inexpensive padlock can be fed through the plug prongs to prevent tools from being plugged in.

While on the subject of children, one of the greatest things you can do is pass on your knowledge of woodworking to them. Encourage them to work with you in the workshop. First and foremost, teach them to respect the inherent dangers involved in the handling of all tools and other materials. Teach them to respect the tools and appreciate their usefulness and emphasize to them that adult supervision is required. With proper guidance, you'll have your daughter or son making compound miters and dovetail joints in no time at all.

FINISHING

There are a variety of wood finishing materials that have uses in the workshop.

Lacquer is available as a brushing or spraying compound and has much the same characteristics as shellac. Lacquer is, however, faster drying, and therefore coats of lacquer can be built up much more quickly. It does take many more coats of lacquer to build it up to a thickness similar to that achieved with shellac or varnish. If you are going to brush it on, use only the very best brushes because it easily leaves brush marks.

Linseed oil is available either raw or boiled. Do not use raw linseed oil. Boiled linseed oil was used for many years because it was cheap and readily available. It leaves a solid, but not too hard film on wood that is easy to repair, but is not recommended as a final finish.

Polyurethane (also known as Varathane) is a synthetic material that is more properly called a plastic finish. It's available in high-gloss, medium or satin finishes. Polyurethane is easily applied, dries quickly and can be used to smooth out brush marks. This is certainly my choice for a durable finish.

Sanding sealers are fast-drying solvent-release compounds that are used on raw wood to fill in between the raised grain of the wood prior to the application of a finish product. Do not use varnish or oils on top of sealers. If the sealer is sanded after it is applied, it will produce a very smooth surface. Sealers are excellent for fine-grained woods, but not for open-grained woods such as oak.

Shellac is a natural resin that is available in flakes for mixing with alcohol or as a ready mix in either clear (white) or orange. There is very little difference between clear and orange, except that the orange will leave the wood slightly colored, will keep a little longer, and is slightly more resistant to moisture.

Shellac bonds to itself readily and will accept lacquer quite well, though oils and varnish will not adhere to it. It can be polished to almost any sheen, from satin to French polish. It is only used for finishes for interior use and should not be used for bar or countertops or any surface that is susceptible to alcohol spillage.

Traditional varnish, which is made from natural resins, is sometimes hard to find. Today's varnish is much different in that it contains synthetics and hardeners. If it's a hard, durable finish that you want, consider using polyurethane.

Tung oil dries to a harder film than linseed oil and is more moisture-resistant. There seems to be some debate over its usefulness as a final finishing product. I generally reduce it with mineral spirits, apply several coats, and then sand it with 0000 steel wool. This gives it more body and depth.

finishing, long workpieces

When finishing or painting long pieces like moldings and such, storing them for drying can be a problem in a small shop. Tighten a couple of pipe clamps to the edge of your workbench. Use some small bar clamps and tighten them on the pipes. You now have a make-shift drying rack.

finishing, raking light

Before that final sanding and finish application, use a portable light such as a halogen lamp on a low angle on your workpiece. This low angle will emphasize any sander swirls or other defects that need to be corrected.

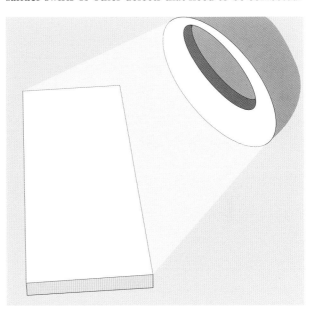

finishing, safety procedures

Most wood-finishing materials are either flammable or toxic. Extreme care should be exercised when working with them. Never use them near sparks or open flames, and always use an appropriate respirator, one that is rated for toxic fumes or odors. Use these materials only in well-ventilated areas.

There are two very important points that aren't usually addressed on the containers of finishing materials. The first is concerned with the empty containers of these materials. Call your city waste disposal department and they will advise you on how to dispose of these containers. The second point concerns how to dispose of the rags you've been working with. Never toss the used rags into a waste bin. Always hang them, fully open, up to dry in a cool, well-ventilated area, for example, on the clothesline. Used rags left in a pile will spontaneously combust.

Laws passed in both Canada and the United States seriously restrict the toxicity and flammability of consumer products such as these (VOC's Volatile Organic Compounds). There are a number of wood-finishing products now available that address these concerns. There are water-based contact cement, wood stains, and varnishes on the market that are safer to use than the older materials.

grain raising

To ensure a smooth finish on your wood project, spray a fine mist of water on the wood before the final sanding. This will raise the grain and the final sanding will smooth it out. The wood is now ready for staining and the stain will penetrate more evenly.

knots, hiding

Knots in pine or spruce have a tendency to "bleed" through paints and other finishes. To prevent this from happening, brush or spray a few coats of shellac on the knots. The shellac will seal the knots and prevent the resin from bleeding through.

paint

There are a variety of paints available for many different situations. Glossy paints have traditionally been oil-based and include a resin to give them a hard-wearing quality. Water-based gloss paints are available.

An alternative to ordinary gloss, non-drip paint is of a jelly-like consistency and is easier to use if not overloaded onto a brush and adequately "laid off" on the surface. It is ideal if you have difficulty in painting without drips falling from the brush, as its consistency allows a "blob" of paint to be picked up by the brush and then applied to the surface where it is spread out normally. Non-drip paint *will* produce runs if too much paint is applied and not adequately laid-off. This is especially true when painting in corners (such as in panel doors).

Modern emulsion paints are water-based, with vinyl or acrylic resins added to make them more hard-wearing than traditional emulsions. This results in varying degrees of sheen in the finish; as the shine increases, the paint tends to be more hard wearing. The ranges usually include matt, eggshell, silk, satin and full gloss.

Although normally thought of as used for internal walls and ceilings, there are water-based types of emulsion paint specially produced for woodwork.

These are easy to apply but do not give the same hard-wearing qualities as oil-based paints. Emulsion paint is the most popular paint for walls and ceilings due to the fact that it is water-based and has less smell, dries comparatively quickly, and is easy to apply.

Primer is the first coating of paint applied to a surface. Primer paints may be oil-or water-based and are used to seal unpainted surfaces to prevent covering coats of paint from soaking in. The appropriate type of primer should be used for the surface being painted, that is, if the surface is wood, metal, plaster or tiles. There are some "all-purpose primers" available that are designed for two or more of these surfaces. An undercoat is applied on top of the primer. It is usually oil-based, and should be of the correct color to provide the right color base for the finishing coats.

paint brushes, bargain

Inexpensive paint and stain brushes may be found at woodworking tool suppliers in quantities at reasonable prices. The problem with them is that they may shed some bristles; and that is annoying. However, if you use a hair comb on them and flap them on a table edge before using them they will do a great job.

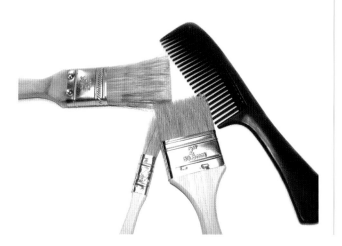

paint brushes, cleaning

Cut an X in the plastic top of a coffee can. Force the paintbrush handle through the cut. Half fill the empty coffee can with the appropriate brush cleaner or solvent and then put the cover back on. Now, the brush will stay suspended and you can swish the brush back and forth without worrying about splashing.

paint brushes, cleaning

This method involves an economical way of cleaning your paintbrush after the paint has hardened. Usually, cleaning paintbrushes after the paint has hardened on them means using a fair quantity of brush cleaner. You pour the cleaner into an old coffee can or similar-sized container. Then you let the brush soak overnight. The next day you end up disposing of the used cleaner.

This more economical way of doing it consists of using old, small oval-shaped glue bottles. They are usually just big enough for most paintbrushes to fit into. Cut the top off just below the shoulder. Now, set the brush in the container and then pour in your brush cleaner until it covers the bristles. A lot less cleaner is required.

Most paintbrushes have a hole in the lower part of the handle for supporting the brush so that the bristles don't touch the bottom of the container. If yours doesn't, drill one. A ¼" hole will do nicely. A small dowel or a piece of coat hanger will support the brush. By doing this, you will double or even triple the amount of brushes that can be cleaned with a standard container of brush cleaner

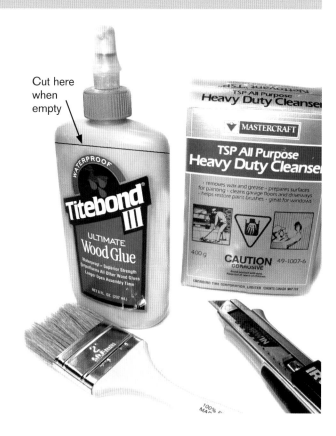

Cut here when empty

paint brushes, cleaning

Don't go to a hardware store and buy any of those expensive paintbrush cleaners that promise to restore your brushes and make them look like new. Instead, purchase a pound or so of trisodium phosphate (TSP) at the same hardware store.

A solution of one pound of TSP mixed in a gallon of water will melt any caked-on paint and soften the brush bristles. For easy reference, here are the rough solutions: 1 pound TSP and 1 gallon of water; 12 ounces TSP and 6 pints of water; 6 ounces TSP and 3 pints of water; 3 ounces TSP and 1½ pints of water; 1½ ounces TSP and 1 pint of water. A little more or less is not crucial. Warm water will work best. The brushes should be left to soak in the solution and should be checked from time to time. The amount of time will depend on just how saturated the brushes are. A second cleaning may be necessary.

paint brushes, homemade

Many of the less-expensive foam paint brushes seem to fall apart well before you have finished your workpiece. Here is a simple way to make your own that will last much longer and will do a better job. Using tongue depressors or popsicle sticks, glue them to Flecto stain applicator pads with craft spray adhesive.

paint brushes, preserving

To preserve your paintbrush for recoating in the next day or two, freeze it. If you are using disposable vinyl gloves while painting, simply grasp the bristles, pull your glove off your hand and over the brush, and put it in your freezer.

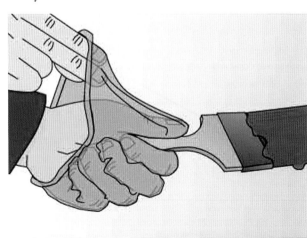

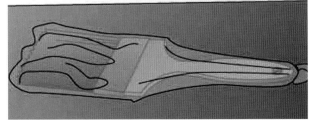

paint brushes, using old

You can make use of old paintbrushes by removing their bristles and metal casings. You are now left with a handle that can be used to spread glue or, if you cut a slot in it you can make a scraper or a spatula. A little imagination is all that's required.

paint, dust-free drying

If you are doing a lot of small-part painting or finishing in your shop, get yourself a used, wardrobe moving carton. These are available at moving companies, and the used ones are much less expensive. The boxes fold for easy storage after use. Hang those painted small parts from the included hanger bar and then close the box. It will keep the items relatively dust-free while they dry

painting, drawer handles

It is almost impossible to paint a small drawer handle without getting paint all over your hands. To prevent this from happening, place a piece of double-faced tape on your paint table and then stick the small parts (drawer handles, knobs, etc.) onto the tape. This will prevent them from moving around as you carefully paint them.

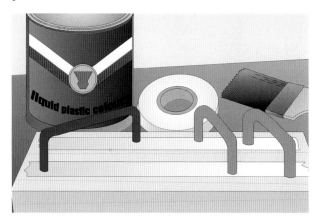

paint, estimating amount

To properly estimate the paint required, do the following: Multiply the length of each wall by the height of the wall in feet. Ignore the doors and windows. Add up the totals. This will give you the total number of square feet for the room. Add 10 percent to the figure. This will take into account those little touch-ups and leave a little left over.

Now, it's time to go to the paint store. You have the information that they require and they will tell you the quantity needed of the type of paint that you want. Be sure to tell them what the wall texture or material is as well.

paint, filtering

From your handy hardware store buy a yard or two of nylon window screening like the kind you find on those aluminum storm doors. Cut a piece just a little larger than your paint can, cut it in half, remove the lid, and tape the piece to the can. An alternate method is cut a piece to fit over the deep end of your roller tray. Now, pour the paint into the tray. If the screen is on the paint can, leave it there but put the cover back on to prevent the paint from drying out. If the screen is on the roller tray, carefully remove and dispose of the screen. This will ensure that any skin or blobs of paint don't get on your brush or roller. It's not necessary to do this with a new can of paint, just with the ones that have been sitting around the basement for a year or two and are only partially full.

paint, full coverage

To paint all sides of a workpiece, drive some 1½" finishing nails through a couple (or more) strips of ½" plywood that are 2" wide × 6" long. Paint or finish the underside first and then set it on the protruding nails. Now, finish the rest of it.

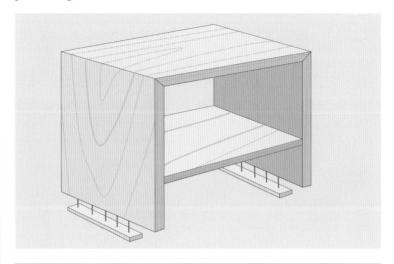

paint, going up a ladder

Up a ladder with a gallon of paint? You know how precarious that can be. Get hold of a dowel or broomstick and put it through the aluminum ladder rung. A large washer forced onto the end of the dowel or even a notch cut into the dowel will hold the wire handle of the paint can relatively secure. Use a bent coat hanger to hold the brush or roller as well.

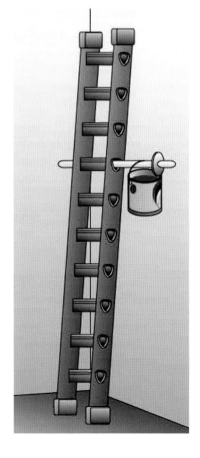

paint, keeping cans clean

Hammering a lid back on a paint can usually splatters the paint all over the place. When you open up that can of paint next time, put a six-inch strip of masking tape over the groove on the inside and outside of the lip. Use this area to scrape the excess paint off the brush and the paint will go back into the can, not the groove. Remove the tape before resealing the paint can.

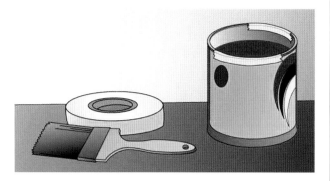

paint, mixing

Before recycling those plastic soda pop bottles, cut the tops off them and put the remaining section on your paint shelf. These small "bowls" will make great disposable containers for mixing small amounts of touch-up paints and finishes. If you drill a couple of small holes up near the top of the bottle, a bent coat hanger will hook it onto a ladder. Oh, save the top section too, it makes a handy funnel.

paint, mixing

If mixing paint with a mixer or an old eggbeater that fits on a power drill, invariably the paint will spatter. Put your paint can in a plastic bucket that is taller than the can. It will save a lot of clean-up.

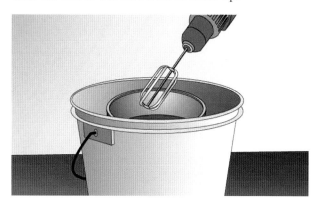

paint, mixing

Although there are many different types of paint mixers on the market, this method is equally effective. I use an old beater from a Mix-Master. This beater is installed in my portable variable speed drill. Starting off very slowly, I gradually increase its speed until the paint is mixed thoroughly. Let the paint drip off the beater, put the beater in thinner or water (depending on the paint), and turn it again for cleaning.

When mixing paint with your portable drill, get a lid from a plastic ice-cream or margarine container that is large enough to cover the top of your paint can. Drill a hole large enough for the beater shaft to fit through, cover the paint can, and start mixing. This will prevent any chance of splattering.

paint, pouring

Stick a piece of wide masking tape to the inside of the inner rim of a new can of paint. (You may have to wipe it dry first.) The tape should be about 4" long and 2" wide. This will make a spout that will keep the inner rim and the outside of the can nearly paint-free.

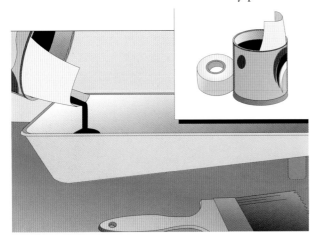

paint rollers, storage

Store your used paint roller overnight if you haven't quite finished the paint job. When it's time to quit for the day use that chip container that you emptied at lunchtime. Cut a small slit down the side for the frame and then put the cover back on. This will keep the roller ready to use in the morning.

paint rollers, prevent sliding

Paint rollers sometimes slide laterally on the roller frame, and that can be annoying. To prevent this, use a file to "score" the wires on the frame. This should keep the roller in place.

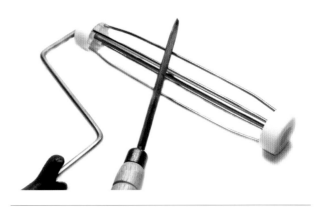

paint roller, cleaning tray

Most of a painter's time is spent in preparing the surfaces for paint and then cleaning up the tool afterward. This technique will save time and money when cleaning up the tools:

Plastic roller tray inserts are fairly expensive. A pack of three is about the same price as a new tray. Your dry cleaner has the answer. The plastic bags that they wrap suits and dresses in make ideal tray covers. Slip the tray halfway into the bag, set it on the floor, and pour in the paint. When you are finished, pour any excess carefully back into the can, roll up the plastic.

paint spray can, cleaning

When you have finished with a can of spray paint and there is still some left in it, remove the spray tip and put it on a can of WD-40 lubricant. Give it a squirt and then replace it back on the paint can. Should the two spray tips not be compatible, use the plastic straw on the WD-40 to clean the paint nozzle. This will keep the nozzle clean for later use.

paint, storing

There is another way to store partially empty cans of paint. Place a plastic shopping bag over the can. Put the top on over the plastic and hammer it on tight. Then, with a pair of scissors or a utility knife cut away the excess bag. This will not only make a better seal but will prevent spatters when you hammer on the top.

paint, steps

Don't get trapped when painting steps. Some people paint one half of the step first and then the second half, but then overlapping will show. Instead, paint every second one on the first day and then the remaining steps on the next day. If they require a second coat, repeat the process but place a flat board on the dry ones as an indicator.

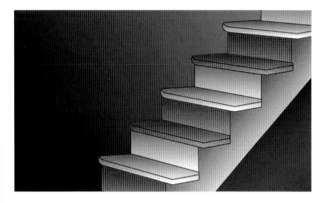

paint, storing

Partially empty paint cans should be stored upside down. This way, any skin that forms will be on the bottom when you next open the can. The skin will usually support the weight of the paint on top of it, so mix it thoroughly but avoid breaking the skin. Also, make sure that the lids are on tight before inverting the paint cans.

paint thinner, recycling

Pour your used paint thinner into clear plastic containers such as soda pop bottles, label them and cap them. After a while you will find that the paint or other materials have settled to the bottom and that the rest of the paint thinner is now clear. Carefully pour the clear paint thinner into another clean container and label it. This re-cycled paint thinner is still effective and may be used again.

refinishing

Your spouse has just come back from a flea market with an "antique" table in the back of the station wagon. It has 10 or 12 coats of paint and varnish on it, so you know what he/she has in mind. Off you go to the workshop.

The first thing to do is to get a scrap piece of plywood or paneling that is two feet larger all around than the table. Set the table on it and move all your refinishing paraphernalia so that it's close at hand. With conventional strippers, the area should be well ventilated. The area temperature should be around 21 degrees Celsius or 72 degrees Fahrenheit for the most effective penetration of any stripper. Rubber, vinyl or latex gloves are mandatory when you are stripping furniture, as are safety glasses. If conventional strippers are used, I recommend the use of any approved respirator.

The materials required are as follows: Old clothes, a selection of finish removal pads (coarse, medium, and fine), a bucket of clean water or easy access to a laundry tub and faucet, a couple of rolls of paper towels, some pieces of scrap foam rubber, a wide putty knife, a copper wire brush, an old toothbrush, mineral spirits (varsol or paint thinner), screwdrivers, a small pry bar, a utility knife and an old plastic pail.

Before starting, I suggest you take a several photos with a digital camera of the piece for both later comparison (it's nice to get a pat on the back once in a while) and to know where all those little pieces of hardware go. Remove all of the hardware pieces and set them in the plastic pail. A mini wonder bar can be used here to carefully remove those parts that are glued on with paint. Use the utility knife to carefully score around some parts to break the paint seal. Pour a little stripper over the parts in the bucket and put them aside. Now, go to work. Follow the manufacturer's directions to the letter when applying the stripper. Use the removal pads and rinse them often in clean water. The putty knife, wire brush, and toothbrush are used for getting into those tight corners and the intricate details or carvings. The paper towels are for the final cleanup. When applying this stripper, try

this technique: Place a plastic container under each leg. The stripper that doesn't adhere will collect in the containers and can be reused. Be sure to empty them back into the original container before you start scraping.

To determine if all the old finish and oils are removed when

refinishing (continued)

you are done, go over the entire piece with mineral spirits and clean paper towels. If there are any traces of the old finish on the paper towel, try one more application.

The tedious part is removing the paint from all of those little hardware parts. The copper brush should speed things up for you.

When you've finished stripping the project, you can see what it looked like when originally built. However, if there are some dark-stained rings on the top or what looks like a cigarette burn, don't fret. Go into the laundry room and get a bottle of laundry bleach. Apply some to the spots. Usually, the rings will disappear, but the burns may only lighten up.

It's time to start the final finish. Determine the type of wood that the table is made of. If you can't identify it, take a sample to a lumberyard, cabinetmaker, or antique dealer. If you don't like the natural color, then stain is the answer. My choices are gel type stains from Flecto or MinWax. These are water-soluble and easily cleaned with a damp cloth.

Before applying the stain, however, try this shortcut: Moisten the end of your finger and press it on the top of the wood. The moistened area will be close to what the unstained color will be with an oil-based clear coat finish. Should you be convinced that the piece needs stain, start applying it. The easiest way that I know of applying stain is to use a scrap piece of foam rubber. Here's another technique: To increase

the brown shades, use dark walnut. To increase the yellow shades, use oak. To increase the orange shades, use maple. To increase the red shades, use mahogany or cherry.

Apply your stain lightly and then use a clean soft cloth and wipe diagonally across the wood grain to help fill in the areas that are missed. Add more coats until the desired density is achieved. A light buffing with a synthetic sanding pad between coats will ensure a smooth finish.

If the natural wood is to your liking, then all that's left to do is apply a protective finish. You can use the methods of the old school wood finishers and start with fillers, conditioners, etc., or you could use the new methods, which I prefer. Whichever you choose, do the insides, edges and underneath parts as well. This will help prevent the wood from expanding or contracting, which will cause warping and splitting later.

Using a high-speed palm sander and 240-grit and finer sandpaper, sand the entire piece. Vacuum the dust off it, then use a tack cloth to wipe up any remaining dust. Apply water-soluble polyurethane with a fine brush or a piece of scrap foam rubber. Use a synthetic (plastic) finishing pad between coats.

Note: Never use steel wool with these products. They are either water-based or have water in them. Any residue from the steel wool may leave rust spots.

After the third and final coat, I like to use boiled linseed oil rubbed in with a fine finishing pad. I let it stand overnight and then wipe it off with a soft cloth dampened with mineral spirits.

One important point: Water-based polyurethane will lighten the finished product and will not darken the grain of the wood. The solvent-based polyurethane product will tend to yellow the work piece, but will enhance the grain. Staining the project will compensate for the color differentials. If you want to change the natural color of the piece before finishing, select from some pastel shades of stain that look like milk paint.

If you are going to use an oil-based stain, the final finish should be a varnish, lacquer or polyurethane. A water-based stain should be followed by a water-soluble polyurethane. Read the instructions on the labels.

A Very Important Note: Do not throw your old saturated rags away in a pile. They may self-combust. Put them outside or lay them flat over a clothesline until they are absolutely dry.

refinishing, removing paint

Here's a quick tip: Trisodium phosphate mixed with water (I pound to I gallon) will remove a coat or two of old paint on furniture. Brush a generous amount of the solution on and allow it to soften. A plastic scraper or dull putty knife will remove the softened paint quite readily. Rinse the cleaner surface immediately afterwards with water and then wipe it dry. A stronger solution may be required for areas with more paint. Rubber gloves and safety goggles should, of course, be worn when working with these materials.

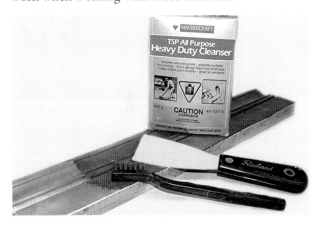

refinishing, spindles

Spindles are always a problem when refinishing furniture. The intricate shapes are difficult to get into without distorting them with scrapers or even sandpaper. The easiest way of stripping them is to put them back into a lathe. Cut a couple of square pieces of scrap wood and attach them to the spindle ends with hot-melt glue; then remount the spindle in the lathe. Sandpaper or even gouges or chisels will make quick work of the old finish.

refinishing, removing glue

White vinegar will soften most hardened glue and make disassembly of furniture easier. Use a wire brush to remove most of it, but be careful as the vinegar may leave a stain where you don't want one. Try it on a test area first.

shellac, use the right type

Which type of shellac should the wood finisher use, natural or de-waxed? For the novice this question may never arise until he/she picks the wrong type. The answer is pretty straight forward. Shellac in its natural state contains wax and if this is the only finish you are going to use then this is the one for you. Should you want to have a more durable finish on top of the shellac, use the de-waxed product. This will prevent a fisheye problem in the finish.

shelves, painting & finishing

You can easily paint, stain, or apply polyurethane (varathane) to your newly made shelves if you have a dozen or so shop-made stacking bars on hand. What are stacking bars? They are H-shaped pieces of wood that are cut from 1×2s and are 10" to 12" long. Before using them, drill holes to facilitate a 2½" finishing nail. Now, when you are ready to finish the shelves, nail a stacking bar to each end. When you have finished one side, just turn it over and do the other. Two additional bonuses: You can now stack your freshly finished shelves horizontally to take up less space when drying, and by stacking them horizontally, you lessen the chances of paint drip or runs.

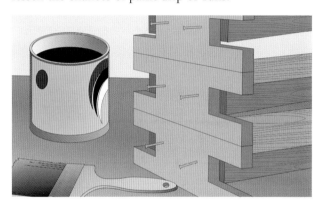

spray finishing & painting

Newspaper or brown paper is usually used with masking tape to mask off areas that you don't want to paint. Newspaper is sometimes difficult to shape in certain areas. Here's an easier method. Use plastic wrap because it will mold better to intricate shapes. You will still need to use the masking tape, but the plastic wrap will cling and the tape will be easier to apply.

spray booth, shop made

Plastic vapor barrier can be used to make a temporary spray-paint booth. Staple the plastic to the ceiling joists and to laths at the floor level. The laths can float free. Make a three-sided "tent" with the plastic at a window opening. An exhaust fan in the window will help dissipate the overspray.

A WORD OF CAUTION: Use only water-based paints in this shop-made booth, as solvent-based fumes and lacquers could be both explosive and toxic.

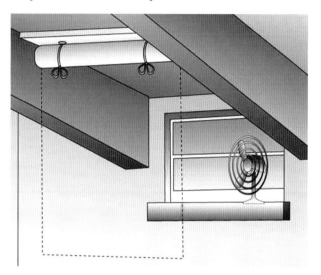

spray gun, filling

Filling a spray gun pot from a gallon finish or paint container can be a messy job at best. Using a trimmed plastic or paper drinking cup will make it less so. Use a sharp knife or a pair of scissors to make the cut as shown in the illustration.

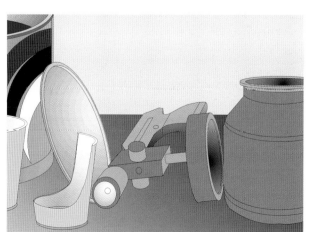

spray paint aid

Using a lazy Susan is one of the best ways of making sure all areas are covered when spray-painting smaller items. To make the lazy Susan, purchase a 12" bearing plate at your home improvement center and install it on a piece of ½" × 24" diameter plywood. Drive some 2" finishing nails partially into the plywood to keep your project raised to prevent paint buildup at the bottom of it.

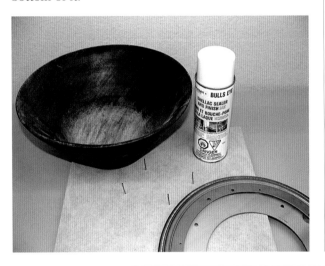

stain, aniline dye

The next time you do any wood staining try using aniline dyes instead of the traditional oil-based or gel type stains. The aniline dyes can provide you with a great variety of colors that can be mixed to your liking. Aniline dyes are a powder and are mixed with water, so, after they are applied, an additional sanding of your work piece will be required due to the raised wood fibers.

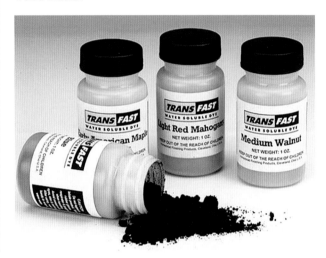

stain, applying

A quick and easy way to evenly apply an oil-based or water-soluble wiping stain is with a pump-type sprayer. They are usually available at your local hardware stores for a few dollars. The beauty of these sprayers is that the stain is applied uniformly. If properly applied, there will be no overlapping or dark spots to worry about. And there's a bonus: You will use a lot less stain. Before using the sprayer on your work piece, try it on a piece of scrap so that the nozzle can be properly adjusted. What you want is a fine mist that will spread evenly. Hold the sprayer 12" to 15" away from the surface. Do about one square foot at a time. Spray it and then wipe it down. A slight overlap on the next section will blend the stain. Do not saturate the board with the spray. Very thin applications are better. This will give you a better idea as to the density and coverage for the desired end result. A word of caution: Do this in well-ventilated areas and wear the recommended safety gear.

stain, applying

Instead of using a paintbrush to apply wood stain which you will have to clean afterwards, use scraps of foam rubber or pieces of an old sponge. When you are done, just throw them away.

stain, story board

Keeping a record of the finishes (paints and/or stains) that you have used on various projects is easy on this finish board. Cut a piece of ½" plywood 24" × 8" like the illustration. Score the panel divisions with a sharp knife. Paint or stain each of the panels with the relevant finish and then write the name of the project, paint or stain mix number, date and other information on it.

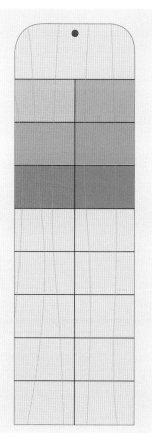

stain, storage

Some finishes and paints can leave a hardened residue in the lip of the can that makes reopening a sometimes difficult task. This can be solved by putting plastic food wrap over the top of the can before sealing.

steel wool, dust removal

Steel wool is great for cleaning projects between finishing coats, but it does leave little specks of steel behind. To make sure you have gotten all of them, cover a magnet with a piece of felt and lightly wipe the surface down.

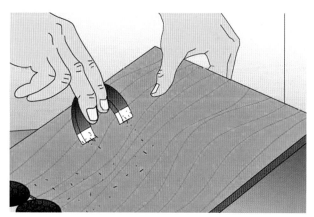

steel wool, using

Although steel wool will leave rust marks on water based stains and finishes, there are still plenty of applications where this inexpensive abrasive can be used. Coarse grades are particularly useful in conjunction with paint and varnish remover. Steel wool is excellent at removing the softened finish.

water stains, removing

To remove water stains from finished wood, try a little oxalic acid (Zud) mixed with water. Use a Q-tip to apply it only to the stain area. Try it on a sample piece first to see if you have the right water/acid strength. When the spot is removed, rinse the area with washing soda and water. Wait for a day or two before refinishing the piece to match the original finish.

water stains, removing

Dark water stains on unfinished wood can easily be removed with oxalic acid stain remover compounds. Applying it with a wet sponge will restore the wood to its original condition.

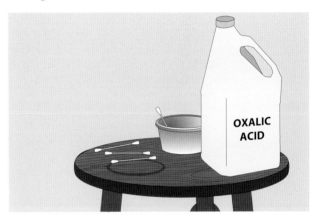

wood, aging

To give wood that "aged" look, sandblast it and then stain it with a product like MinWax's Driftwood oil stain. If you already have a compressor, a sandblasting attachment is an inexpensive option.

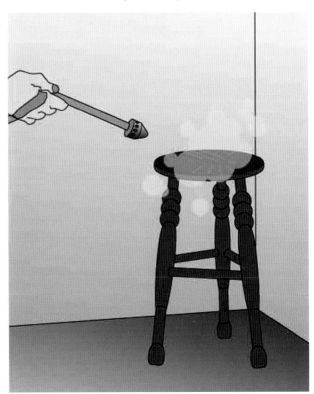

FURNITURE

buffing

A paint roller makes an excellent buffer for wood or metal projects. You can cut it to size to fit on a sanding drum and then mount it in a drill press or you can leave it the way it is and use it on an oscillating sander.

box lids, cutting

One other way to safely cut the cover off a box is to glue some interior supports to the box with a hot melt glue gun. After cutting the cover, the supports are easily removed and will prevent any binding when cutting.

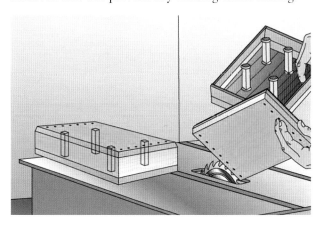

box lids, cutting

When making covered boxes, it is best to make them in one piece as a closed box. Once built, it is easier to then cut the top portion off to use as a cover. This will not only make the job easier, but will match the grain for the cover. The problem with doing this on a table saw is that the final cut for the top portion will "bind" in the saw blade. Here's a way to prevent it from happening. Adjust your saw blade to leave 1/16" or even 1/32" of wood still attached to the box all around. A sharp utility knife and a bit of sanding will clean it up.

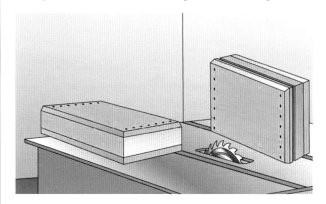

brackets, bed frame

Make your own bed frame brackets using short pieces of shelf standards recessed and screwed into the bedpost uprights. Use the shelf bracket screwed to the bed frame to secure it to the bedpost.

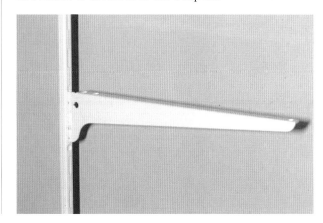

cabinets, installing

You can install upper kitchen cabinets by yourself! It will take a little bit of wiggling but if you have those one-handed bar clamps where you can reverse one end, these will make perfect "jacks" for putting the cabinets into position. Simply brace the cabinet back against the wall that they are to be mounted on and wiggle the compressed stretcher bar clamps under the cabinet. As you squeeze the clamp handles the cabinet will rise.

dimples, removing

Trust me, this technique has nothing to do with cosmetics or facials. The types of dimples that I am referring to are the ones that are inadvertently made by the slip of a hammer or the dropping of some heavy object on your work piece. There are two methods for removing these dimples. The first is to place a wet rag on top of the dent and let it stay there for a few hours. If that doesn't work, try using a steam iron. Apply lots of steam and heat, but be careful that you do not scorch the wood. Both of these methods should work, but they will raise the grain on the wood. After the area has dried out, a little sanding with a very fine-grit sandpaper will bring it back.

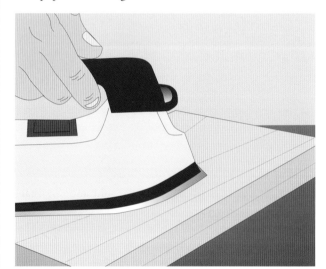

drawers, childproofing

Young, curious hands always seem to wander into things that they are not supposed to, like a drawer that contains sharp tools. To prevent this, make a lock for the drawer that doesn't look like a lock. Hinge a narrow strip of wood to the bottom front of the drawer so that it drops down just behind the front drawer frame. Drill a finger hole into the dust panel below so the lock can be released.

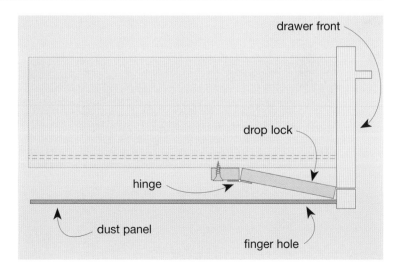

drawers, childproofing

A simple way to keep tiny hands out of a drawer that contains things that you don't want them to get into is to drill a small hole through the bottom of the drawer. Drill the hole near the front of the drawer and then drop a nail through the hole. The drawer underneath will allow you to push the nail up to release the drawer.

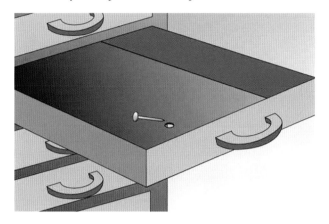

drawer handle jig

It's an old story. You are putting handles on that twelve-drawer dresser that you just built and you realize that measuring, drawing lines, and punching starter holes on each and every drawer is a very tedious job. Try this technique: Cut a piece of polystyrene, available through a plastics wholesaler, to the exact size of your drawer. Measure and place marks on the polystyrene and then drill the required-size holes in it. Tape this template to the drawer and drill away.

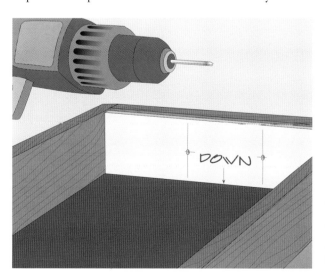

drawer handle, installing

Draw lines diagonally from corner to corner to find the exact center of the drawer. This will provide you with a reference point even if the drawer pulls are not placed in the drawer face centers.

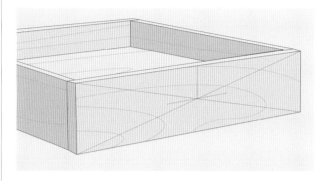

drawer handle jig

This drawer handle jig will work if all the drawers are the same size and the handle positions are in the same place on each drawer. If this is not the case, however, try this template: Again, using polystyrene, cut a piece that is 12" wide × the height of your highest drawer. Find the middle of the plastic and draw a line from top to bottom. Now, find the spacings of the drawer handles. If all the handles are going to be one inch down from the drawer top, for example, drill holes in the plastic accordingly. If some are going to be centered, repeat the above procedure. I drilled holes on ½" centers so that the jig can be used on almost any drawer face using the standard 3" handle spacing. Now all I have to do is to line up the centerline with the drawer, make my mark with an awl, and proceed to drill the holes.

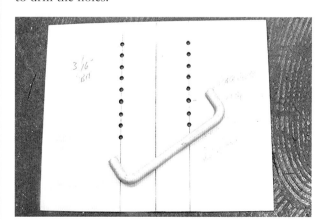

hinges, installing

Installing small cabinet hinges can be made easier if you position them correctly and then put a small dab of hot glue on the holes. This will keep them in position while you either drill starter holes or to set the screws.

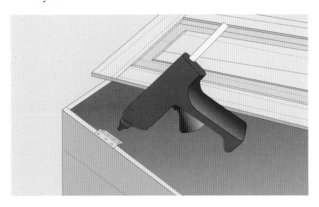

hinges, piano

Most woodworkers that use continuous or piano hinges use a hack saw to cut them to size. This is difficult in most cases as the hinge is flimsy and will "chatter" when cutting it. To get a smooth and chatter-free cut, I use my Dremel motor tool with a cut-off wheel attached. Be careful, the hinge will be hot.

legs, leveling scribe

Remember the dining table that ended up being a coffee table? You keep cutting a piece off one leg to make it level. Never again. Here's a shop aid, made from shop scrap, to eliminate the wobble in tables and chairs. Glue and screw a couple of pieces that are about 3" square, so they form an L shape. Cut a 3"- diameter wheel. Drill a hole in the middle of the wheel and a corresponding hole in the middle of the vertical part of the L. Drill a counter bore at ¼" inch in from the edge of the wheel. Install a drywall (Gyproc) screw in this so that about ⅛" to ¼" of the screw protrudes. Now, recess a carriage bolt through the center holes and fasten it with a washer and a wing nut. Your leveling jig is ready to use. Set your table or chair on a level surface. Rotate the wheel until the protruding screw (scribe) is level with the shortest leg. Tighten the wing nut and use the scribe to mark the other legs for cutting. Voila, no more wobble.

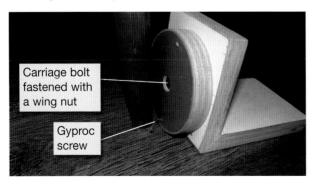

Carriage bolt fastened with a wing nut

Gyproc screw

legs, repairing

Round, dadoed or tapered legs for tables or chairs often become loose due to the drying of the wood and/or the glue. To repair the loose legs, most of us remove them, clean them off, and reinstall them with new adhesive. Maybe the following is a better method: Run a band-saw cut the length of the dadoed end. The kerf is usually ¹/₁₆" so drill a hole at the end of the kerf that is ⅛" in diameter. The purpose of this is to relieve the kerf and deter the leg from splitting further. Before reinstalling the leg, insert a small wedge into the kerf and trim the edges flush. Leave ¼" to ½" sticking out on top. Add the glue and hammer the leg home. The wedge will spread the kerf when the leg is hammered all the way in.

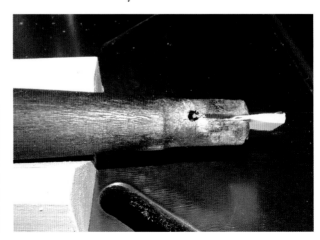

HOUSEHOLD

door edges, sanding

Sanding or planing door edges can be a frustrating experience. The doors have a tendency to wobble, making the job somewhat difficult. A pair of squeeze-type bar clamps placed at the door ends will help stabilize the door.

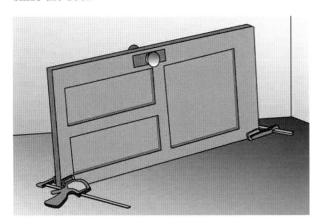

door, shim for installing

Reinstalling a door after making adjustments usually requires some shims to brace it or to raise it slightly to fit the hinge pin. Don't go out and buy a package of shims, use the tools at hand. You probably have a chisel and screwdriver right at your fingertips, together they make a fine wedge or shim.

door locks, installing

Installing locksets or deadbolts on doors can sometimes be a problem. Those long screws that go through the door to connect the two parts usually wobble around for awhile before they reach the target. An easier way of ensuring that they get to that target the first time is through the use of ordinary drinking straws. The best ones to use are the "milkshake" type because they have a wider diameter. Slit them so that they will fit through the screw holes and they will act as channels to guide the screws. You can then tighten up the lockset; the straws will crush themselves and will not interfere with the lockset operation.

door striker, installing plate

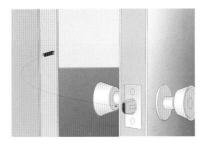

Installing the striker plate when hanging doors has always been a little difficult, until now. Next time you are hanging doors, be they cabinet or entry doors, try this: After the doors are hung, rub a little lipstick on the latch and close the door. The lipstick mark will transfer onto the frame and indicate exactly where to place the striker plate. In the event that you don't have lipstick, you might try chalk-line powder or tape a piece of pencil carbon paper to the latch. Double-faced tape will work best.

garden tools, storing

Gained a little weight around the middle? Don't throw that old belt away! To prevent hoes, rakes and such from falling down in your shed, screw your old leather belt to the wall and simply buckle them up.

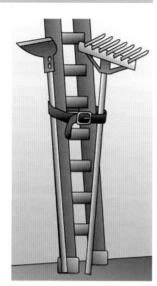

shelf brackets, making

Making fancy scroll-sawn shelf-brackets is easy if you are just making one. Unfortunately, most shelves require at least two. There might be the occasion when you want to make a set of shelves all with the same style brackets. Here's how it's done. Use a thick piece of stock. The thickness is determined by the thickness of each bracket × the number of brackets required. Draw the pattern on the surface and cut it out on your band saw. Now, set the fence on your band saw to the desired thickness of the brackets and proceed to resaw. Here is another tip. It's pretty difficult to find wood stock that is 6" or 8" thick. The answer is to laminate (glue and clamp) several pieces together. When resawing, though, make sure that the glue joints are somewhere near the middle of the brackets.

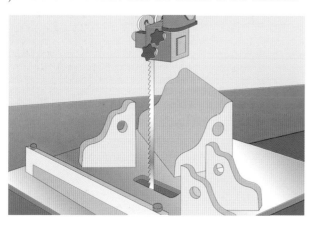

picture frames

Occasionally we are asked to make a picture frame or two, and they are generally easy to do. However, they usually require those special diamond-shaped "points" to keep everything within the frame. Trying to squeeze these into hardwood such as oak can be a problem. An easier way is to use hot-melt glue. Run a tiny bead around the perimeter and everything will be nice and snug.

shelves, making

The next time you are making shelves for that bookcase that your spouse wants, this technique will save you time, energy and clamps. Let's say the shelves are made of pine and you want to have a ½" solid-walnut nosing on them. Try this: Cut your solid nosing stock 1⅛" inches wide × whatever thickness your shelves are. Lay your shelves flat, face to face. Place the solid stock between the front edges of the shelves and glue and clamp them together. When the glue has set, gear up your radial arm saw or your table saw to rip down the middle of the solid stock. That extra ⅛" is for the saw blade kerfs. Normally, you would need two bar or pipe clamps on each shelf. Now, two clamps are used for gluing up two shelves.

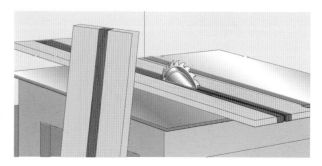

JOINERY

bevel-cutting, band saw

Whenever you are making any bevel cuts on a band saw, use a fence. It does not matter if you use one that comes with the machine or if you make one out of ¾" plywood. The important thing is that a fence should guarantee a straight and true bevel cut. Needless to say, if you are beveling a scroll cut, the fence will be useless. If your tool does not have a fence, the easiest way of making a temporary one is to use a narrow piece of straight-edged plywood clamped to your saw's table when required; making a beveled cut with the fence in place. Cut an irregular beveled pattern without the fence.

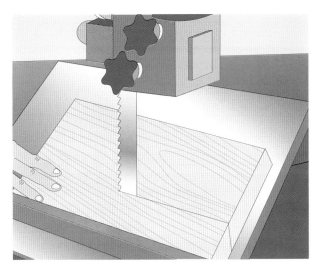

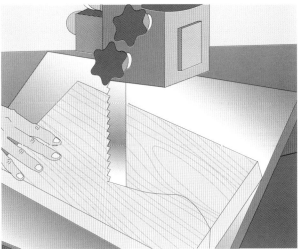

butt joints, strengthening

Screwing butt joints in MDF or other manufactured wood material are generally very weak. Drill into one edge of the MDF to accept a short length of dowel. Drill a pilot hole into the side of the dowel first and make a pencil mark showing the position of the pilot hole. Now, when screwing and gluing the butt joint the dowel will reinforce and greatly strengthen that otherwise weak joint.

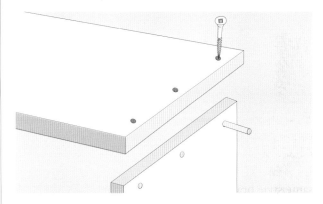

dowel joints

Dowel joints can be among the most secure joints if properly used. The glue with dowel joints must be allowed to spread, and this can't be done with a solid dowel. Special glue-joint dowels are considerably more expensive than just straight dowels. Make your own custom-fitted glue-joint dowels. With a triangular steel file, etch a "thread" into your full-length dowel and then cut it to size for your project. The "thread" allows the glue to spread throughout the joint, and a slight rounding off of the ends makes it even better. (Lines exaggerated for clarity)

edge joining, gluing

Gluing up edge joined table tops can be made easier with a couple of lengths of aluminum angle iron. Invert the angles on the ends of the table top and clamp them to keep the joined boards flush and to prevent any bowing due to the cross-positioned bar or pipe clamps.

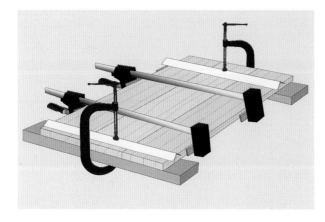

joints, identifying

Suppose you are working on a butcher-block-type table. The thickness planer has been turned off and you are setting up your pieces for gluing. Before you dismantle the setup, get out your pencil. Mark a large V across the setup pieces. Now, if the phone rings and your youngster decides to play with the blocks while you are talking, reassembly will only take seconds.

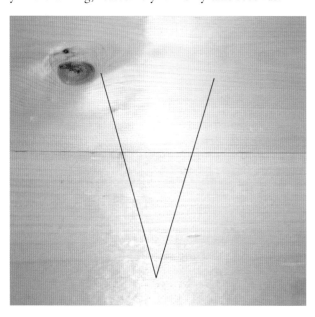

holes, enlarging

To enlarge a hole that you have already drilled, find a dowel or a square piece of scrap that is the size of the drilled hole. Find the center of it and then cut it off to the thickness of your work piece. Insert it into the hole and then proceed to drill with the correct size bit. Make sure that your work piece is well secured to your table.

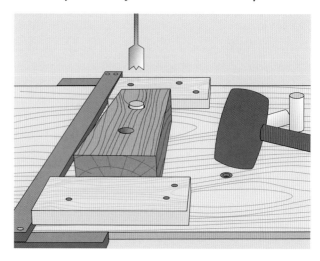

miters, gluing correctly

When gluing up miter cuts you must remember that you may be putting glue on the end grain of wood. The glue will quickly be absorbed into the grain and will not provide a secure glue joint. You must seal the wood first by mixing equal parts of water and your (PVA) glue and then 'paint' the joint. When the sizing dries, apply the final full-strength glue and clamp.

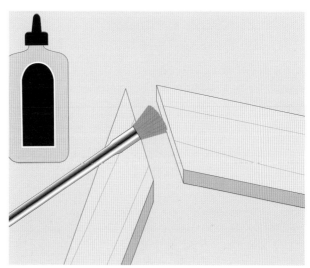

miters, handmade

Here's a magical trick to make a moulding miter cut without the benefit of a miter box and one that will definitely impress your woodworking friends. Set your handsaw so that you can see the mirror image of the piece you are cutting on the blade of the saw. When your saw is exactly at 45° the image will appear as a 90° right angle.

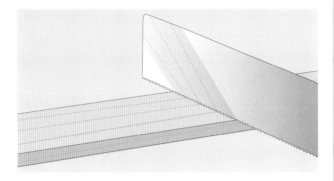

tenons, making round

Making round tenons from square stock on either a table saw or a radial arm saw would seem to be quite a challenge. Here is an easy way of doing it. Insert the square stock into an appropriately sized PVC or ABS pipe so it fits snugly. Leave the desired tenon length, plus an inch, exposed. Raise the table-saw blade to the appropriate height and, using your miter gauge as support, butt the piece up against your fence. That extra inch will keep the saw blade away from the fence, and it can be cut off later. Now, you can make your cuts, but do not rotate the piece into the moving saw blade; back it off the blade and then rotate it. Move the fence accordingly for each successive pass.

miters, hand cutting

Tight-fitting miters for picture frames are usually cut in a miter box. The problem with a lot of the inexpensive miter boxes is that their sides wear out, which affects the accuracy and the tight fit of the miters. Don't throw the miter box out just yet. Make your cuts in it. Remove the pieces and clamp them to a builder's square. Using a backsaw, carefully saw through the joint and stop just before touching the square. Remove the builder's square and saw the rest of the joint. Be sure to mark the corners of the pieces, because your handsaw cut may not have been truly perpendicular and that joint may not fit in another position. This may seem like a lot of trouble to go through, but the end result will be a miter joint without any gaps.

tenons, tightening

If those tenons seem too loose, they are easily fixed through the use of veneer. Cut the veneer to fit the cheeks and glue them in place. Shave or sand them to fit. Be sure that the veneer grain runs the same as the tenon.

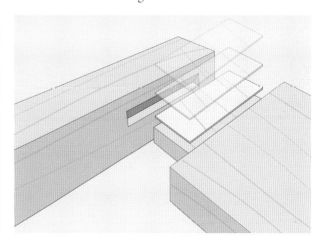

MATERIALS

abrasives

(For more abrasives information, refer to the Tools and Techniques sections.)

The term "abrasives" is a generic one that covers a wide variety of products that remove material. These include powders such as pumice, emery and rottenstone. The term also includes sandpaper in all of its various forms: Sheets, discs, drums, pads and belts. The sheets and discs can be adhesive-backed or hook-and-loop discs (that are more conveniently installed).

Steel wool is a form of abrasive as well and is available in seven grades from coarse to extra fine. The grades start from No. 4 (coarse) to No. 0000, which is extra-fine. Synthetic materials have all but replaced steel wool because the residue from steel wool will leave rust spots when using water-based wood stains and finishes.

abrasives, synthetic

Synthetic adhesives have taken over the roles of sandpaper and steel wool for finishing and between-coat sanding. Among many brands are Bear-Tex by Norton and Scotch-Brite by 3M. These materials resemble pot scrubbers and work very well as finishing abrasives. There's very little residue to worry about. They do a clean job, especially between finishing coats, and do not leave any rust or black spots. These synthetics are not designed for heavy stock removal; they are intended as finishing abrasives only.

abrasives, synthetic - Bear-Tex

Bear-Tex is a nonwoven web of nylon fibers that are impregnated with an abrasive grain (either silicon carbide or aluminum oxide) and then bonded with synthetic resins. The main advantage is that Bear-Tex may be used in either wet or dry sanding situations. These products are available in a wide range of grades. Norton uses two grading systems. The more accurate one uses the actual mesh number and grit size impregnated into the pad. The finest grit size is 1,000 and the coarsest 40, a system not unlike normal abrasive (sandpaper) grading, though a number 40 Bear-Tex pad will be considerably less abrasive than number 40 sandpaper. The other system that Norton uses is a simplified grading system: Micro-Fine (MF), Ultra-Fine (UF), Very Fine (VF), Fine (F), Medium (M) and Coarse (C). Bear-Tex is available in ⅜"- thick sheets of various sizes. A utility knife or scissors will easily cut the product to the size desired. Advantages include: These products will work on a sander equipped with a hook-and-loop type pad without any modification; and they will work well in sanders that have "through-the-pad" dust pickups.

abrasives, synthetic - Durite screen

Another type of synthetic abrasive is Durite™ screen by Norton. This is a product that is primarily designed for the drywall and plaster trades for smoothing joints. The substrate (backing) is a synthetic screen. The screen is impregnated with a 120-or I5O-grit abrasive. Durite is only available in a die-cut form that fits a drywall sander. However, this happens to be about one third of a normal sheet of sandpaper, so it will fit many orbital sanders. The main advantage of this product is that it is a screen and is therefore extremely porous. As a result, when the screen is used with a very hard abrasive, it will last about five times as long as sandpaper. Try it on your finishing sander. Durite is particularly effective when working at the lathe.

acrylic

Acrylic is fun to work with. You can saw, drill, rout, bend and sand it. Here are a few tips you may want to follow when working with this material:

1. Never store acrylic in direct sunlight. The protective paper that's on it will dry up and become difficult to remove.
2. Leave the protective paper on until your project is finished. This will help prevent scratches to the surface.
3. Almost any drill bit may be used on acrylics, as long as it is sharp. Make sure, though, that you have a piece of scrap wood under it and that you drill very slowly, using light pressure.
4. You can cut acrylic with a band saw, but use a blade with the most teeth to the inch. When using a circular saw, also use a blade with the most teeth.
5. To bend acrylic, it be heated in boiling water, in an oven set at low heat or with an electric bender. An electric bender is a tool with two heating elements. Place the acrylic between the two heating elements, wait a moment, and then bend the acrylic. It gets very hot when the above methods are used, so be very careful when handling it. The protective paper should be removed before heating.
6. Sand the edges of acrylic with fine sandpaper or emery cloth. To get a clear edge on the plastic, sand the edge and then run a flame over it. Do this with a propane blowtorch. Make light, frequent passes along the edges. This will leave the edge with a mirror-like finish. Try this out on scrap before doing your workpiece. If the acrylic starts to ignite, blow it out immediately or douse it in water.

acrylic, bending

Acrylics or styrenes can be bent in many ways. Here are three. In the first method, using a propane blowtorch with a pencil-thin flame aimed at the desired crease will soften ⅛" or ¼" acrylic or styrene enough to make a bend in the material. Do not concentrate the flame in one spot, but wave it back and forth across the workpiece and do both sides. The workpiece should be hanging over a straight edge at the bending point. An electric heat gun or hair dryer is another method for heating and bending, but it will take longer to bend acrylics or styrenes in thicknesses over ⅛". The third method involves baking (that's right, baking) the plastic. Use a clean cookie sheet. Lay the workpiece on it, turn up the oven to about 200 degrees, leave the oven door ajar and turn on the exhaust fan. The workpiece will soften like rubber and can be placed into a precut mold. Oven mitts are used for this operation.

acrylic, cutting

To cut Plexiglas, polystyrene and most other plastics up to ¼" thick, score the plastic lightly at first with a scratch awl or other sharp-pointed tool. Repeat the scoring a couple of times using progressively heavier pressure. Align the scribed mark on the edge of your workbench with the scribed face up. Now, holding it securely, bend the material down until it snaps. Practice this a couple of times on some scrap material before trying it on your workpiece.

acrylic, removing paper

An easy way to remove the protective paper is to start at one corner. Start rolling the paper off with a broom handle or a dowel, depending on the size of the piece. If the material has been cut, the edges of the paper may tend to stick, so proceed slowly.

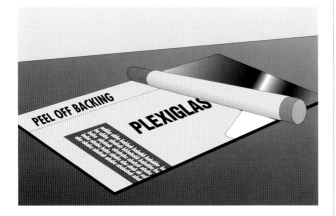

acrylic, safety

Working with plastics poses the same safety hazards as working with wood. When sawing, you must wear a dust mask because the dust is extremely fine, is an irritant to the mucous membranes and some forms of plastic could be toxic. Do not smoke or allow sparks or an open flame anywhere near your work.

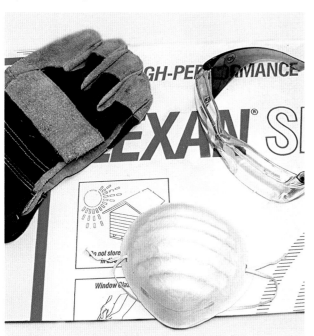

acrylic, marking to cut

Sometimes, when you work with acrylic, you will find that the protective paper has been removed or that the supplier has used a blue polyethylene protector. How do you mark the acrylic for measuring? A pencil won't do, and an awl will leave a scratch right where you don't want it. Try this technique: Your stationary store or art-supplies dealer has water-soluble overhead projection markers in a rainbow of colors and a variety of point sizes. Get a couple of dark-colored ones with fine points. Now, make your lines. A little glass cleaner and a soft cloth will wipe away any errant marks.

acrylic, welding

Acrylic is cold-welded; that is, a liquid acrylic solvent is used to bond the pieces together and the solvent is applied with a hypodermic syringe. Care should be taken when doing this operation because the needle is sharp. Use safety gloves and glasses. The pieces to be "welded" should be clamped or taped together and must be close-fitting. Any gaps will weaken the joint. Inject the solvent into the joint only until you see it fill the seam, because any surplus will leak out and permanently damage the surrounding area. Once it's done, let the piece sit for an hour or so before removing the clamps or tape. Store the solvent and the hypodermic needle in a safe place.

adhesives, applying

Old venetian blind slats make excellent glue spreaders; just cut them into manageable pieces.

adhesives, cleaning bottle

Glue bottles with those spreader tips that snap closed are sometimes not a snap to open. Glue usually cakes in the small opening that renders that spreader tip useless. Remove the screw cap and use a long dental pick to extract the dried glue from the cavity. After the glue is removed, a proper rinsing with warm water is prescribed.

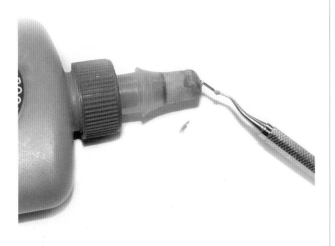

adhesives, applying

Make friends with your doctor. He/she works with tools everyday that can be helpful in your workshop. For example, when the doctor tells you to say aah, ask if you can keep the tongue depressor (and maybe a few more) to use for mixing two-part epoxy glue and for spreading it.

adhesives, economizing

The large one gallon (3.72 liters) of glue is more economical to buy but too difficult to use. Your local "dollar" store sells small mustard and ketchup containers that are the perfect size for the shop and the plastic tip is an excellent applicator.

adhesives, economizing

Glue is more economical if bought in larger containers, but for day-to-day, use fill a small dish detergent bottle with it. The snap-closing top is just the ticket to keep the bottle air tight and leak-free.

adhesives, extending life

The reason that most adhesives lose their effectiveness is the air that gets into the glue bottle as the quantity inside is decreased. To keep the bottle full and displace that air, drop some glass marbles into it until it fills back up. Keep the cap on tight.

adhesives, extending life

Some adhesives such as polyurethanes and cyanoacrylates have a short shelf life after they have been opened. To extend this shelf life I keep mine tightly sealed in a Zip-Lock bag ,making sure that I evacuate the air as I close the bag. This should double the shelf life of the glue. This works well for both cyanoacrylates, white, yellow and other types as well.

adhesives, improving bond

If you are planning to glue up your workpieces, you should do so as soon after machining as possible. Setting them to one side for any length of time may allow dust and even oil to settle on them. Should this happen, a little very fine sanding and then a wiping with denatured alcohol will make them ready for gluing.

adhesives, in cracks

Doctors also use syringes-some with large-diameter needles and some with plastic tips. These work well for applying glue in difficult-to-get-at areas and especially for doing furniture repair.

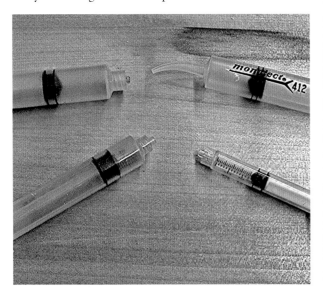

adhesives, in cracks

Sometimes a crack or split will occur in your workpiece when it is least expected. Getting glue in the crack to repair it can be a problem. This idea may help. Dip a length of string in your glue container and then lay the string on the crack. Using a putty knife or other thin tool, force the string down into the crack; then slowly pull out the string. Clamp the piece and wipe up the excess glue.

adhesives, laminate

Don't throw away that old venetian blind just yet; save a dozen or so slats. When you are applying contact cement for laminating, use the slats as spacers to manipulate the top piece into position. Remove them one by one as you press the two pieces together.

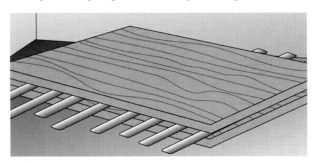

adhesives, protect finish

Before gluing your project together, try lightly rubbing a wax candle on the edges where glue may ooze out and stain your finish. The dried glue should just peel off, and a light sanding will remove any traces of the wax.

adhesives, removing

You've just glued up a small project with white or yellow glue and discovered some seepage of glue on the joints. Try this: If the glue is fresh, some water

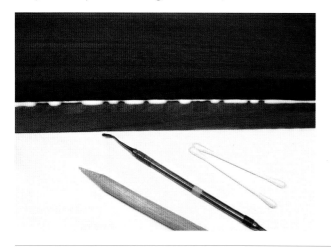

moistened Q-Tips will clean it up. If the glue has been there for a half hour or so, sharpen the end of a ¼" dowel to 45° and proceed to clean it up. Then use moistened cotton swabs in warm water to wipe up the residue. For the conventional solvent-based contact cement, there is a contact cement thinner available from LePage. A Q-Tip dipped in this will work well. If you don't have any of the solvent on hand, try nail-polish remover, the non-oily type. Be sure to wipe the area clean after use. Epoxy-type adhesives should be carefully cut away with a utility knife or a well-sharpened scraper.

Before gluing up a project, put masking tape on the joint's edges. Any seepage should run onto the tape. After clamping the workpiece and after the seepage seems to have stopped, remove the tape.

adhesives, removing

There are a couple of options for removing excess glue or squeeze-out. You can wipe off the excess with a damp cloth or, after an hour or so, you can scrape it off. If the latter is your choice, you probably use a wood chisel that you have dedicated to just this purpose. Well, clean up that chisel and put it back to its intended use. A razor-type window scraper will do a much better job of glue removal and when the blade gets too gooey, simply change the blade.

adhesives, rubber cement

Rubber cement, sometimes called paper cement, makes an excellent temporary adhesive. Use it for stacking stock together for multiple pattern-making or to glue paper patterns for use in scroll sawing. The cement won't stain the wood and is easily removed. For stacking wood pieces together, it should be applied to both surfaces like contact cement. A little prodding with a putty knife will separate the pieces when the cutting is done. To cement paper patterns, apply glue only to the wood surface and apply the pattern while the glue is still wet. When done, the pattern will peel off easily and any residue can be rubbed off with your fingers.

adhesives, selecting

White and yellow glues are water-based and, although they work really well, there are some cautions you should be aware of. The water in these glues swells the joint slightly, so you should wait until the glues have totally cured (read the instructions for times) before doing any sanding or additional milling. The joint will settle down once the glue is cured. Should you not adhere to this warning you may end up with an indent at the joint.

adhesives, small parts

Buying adhesive in larger containers is much more economical, but it has its drawbacks. The containers or plastic bottles are too large to use on individual glue-up jobs. Here's a way of making it easier. Those small pop or soda bottles will hold enough glue to do several small glue-up jobs, but their mouths are too big. Keep the caps; drill holes in them and insert one of those used caulking tube tips through the holes. Make sure the tube tip fits snugly so there are no leaks. A nail, spike, or wire nut will seal the open top of the tip.

adhesives, selecting

Wood species like lignum vitae, cocobolo, teak, ebony, ipé and the like, are extremely oily and as such they require special care when gluing. There are a few adhesive choices; you can use waterproof PVA (Polyvinyl Acetate) glue, polyurethane glue or, should you prefer, you can use interior PVA. You must get rid of the oily surface before applying the glue. This can be accomplished by wiping the joints with denatured alcohol immediately prior to applying the glue.

adhesives, spreading

One method of spreading white glue on larger surfaces is to use a printer's brayer. These are normally used for spreading printer's ink, but they work very well with white glue as well. They come in various sizes and are available at art-supply stores. Wash the brayer off in warm water after use.

adhesives, spreading

Another method of spreading glue is to use a glue spreader. These are inexpensive and available at flooring or ceramic tile dealers. Get the type of glue spreader with the most and the shallowest notches. Rinse it in warm water after using white glue or yellow, or with a suitable solvent if using other types of glue.

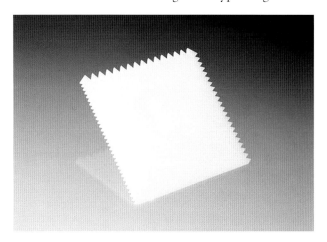

adhesives, spreading

When those foam paintbrushes are worn out, don't throw them away. Cut off the foam portion and keep the handle with that plastic insert. It makes a good glue spreader.

adhesives, spreading

Glue can be spread with old hacksaw blades. Carefully break or cut one in half. Cut six inches or so off an old broom handle. Saw a slot on the end of it on your band saw, mix up some epoxy glue, and glue the top edge of the hacksaw blade into the slot. The result is an effective glue spreader.

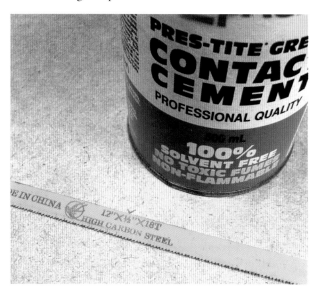

adhesives, spreading

Plumber's acid brushes are inexpensive and available in several sizes. These make great applicators for glue and, if you use water-based glue, they can be washed and used over and over again.

adhesives, storing

Most woodworkers have a variety of wood glues sitting on their workbenches and they are all in an upright position. Drill enough holes in a scrap piece of 2×4 to allow the glue bottles to be stored inverted. The glue will keep better and will be ready to use when stored upside down.

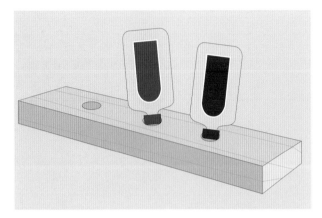

adhesives, squeeze out

Some of the tools your dentist uses are really great for removing excess glue either wet or after it has dried. Your dentist usually tosses these out after multiple uses, so they might as well end up in your workshop. The various shapes of these stainless steel tools can be used in a multitude of other situations as well. For example, cleaning tar and pitch off saw blades and router bits, cleaning out fine detail work when stripping the finish from furniture, applying wood filler in small areas, etc. As you see the various shapes of these tools, you will appreciate their possibilities even more.

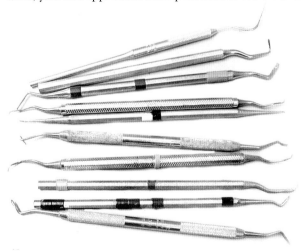

adhesives, storing

Here's a neat, inexpensive and convenient way to store all of those various glue bottles that we tend to accumulate. And, it takes up very little space. Your local dollar store will have those canvas or cloth shoe bags. You know the ones; they hang on the back of a door. Well, the pockets are just the thing for glue bottles and other items.

adhesives, squeeze out

Glue squeeze-out should be cleaned up as soon as it occurs by either scraping it off or, if the glue is water-based, wiped off with a damp cloth. The reason for a quick clean-up is because if the glue crusts over, it blocks any air entering the joint and thus, retards the curing of the glue.

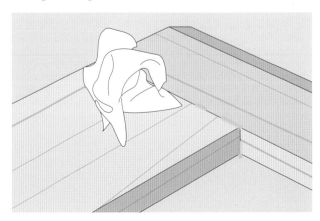

adhesives, thickening

Slowing down the run time for glue! Should you find that your glue is running too quickly, put it in the refrigerator for an hour or so. This will thicken the glue so it flows slower. The cold glue provides you with a longer open time as well.

brass, removing tarnish

To remove tarnish from brass, dip No. 0000 steel wool into white vinegar and scrub the brass clean.

aluminum, grinding

Aluminum can make a mess out of a file or a grinding wheel when used to remove the burr that is left after the aluminum has been cut. Aluminum is soft and the shavings tend to stick in the crevasses of the files. Because of the heat buildup when a grinding wheel is used, the aluminum accumulates and sticks to the wheel. When the latter happens, a good wheel dresser is required. As for the files, a lot of tedious work with a wire brush is needed. Save your money and your time. Your local supermarket sells cans of nonstick cooking spray. A couple of squirts on your grinding wheel and files before use will help prevent clogging.

caulk, bathtub

When recaulking around the inside of a bathtub, make sure that the tub is full of water. Keep the water in it until the caulk has dried to the touch. This will give the caulk a better seal and further ensure that there will be no leaks. Conversely, when removing the old caulk, filling the tub with water will make the job easier and ensure that you get all of the old caulk out.

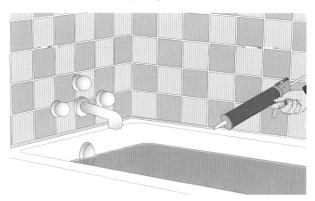

caulk, preventing drying

There is nothing more annoying that having the caulk in a previously opened caulking tube dry up. You place the half-full tube in your gun and discover that nothing will come out. To prevent this, next time you open a tube of caulk and have finished using it, take a large pan-head wood screw, one that is large enough to fit on the inside of the nozzle, and screw it into the nozzle. You can also screw a large electrical wire nut onto the head of the nozzle.

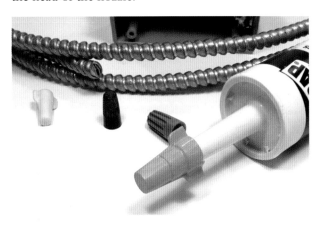

caulk, preventing run-on

To prevent caulking tubes from "running on" after you have released the trigger, tightly wrap the tube in duct tape before inserting it into the gun. This deters the expansion of the tube that occurs because of the pressure exerted on the back of the tube when the trigger is released. To make doubly sure the tube does not run, also release the trigger catch when releasing the trigger.

caulk, smooth bead

To do an effective job of caulking around a bathtub, sink, window or door frame, place a small bead of silicone caulk or other type of caulk around the perimeter. Pour a small amount (about 1 ounce) of liquid dish detergent into a glass or plastic cup along with an equal amount of water. Dip the thumb or middle finger into the liquid and carefully force the caulk into the corners, making sure to dip frequently.

copper pipe, resoldering

I put this great resoldering tip in the book because many of us woodworkers own homes and plumbing is usually the number-one repair problem. If you have to repair a joint in copper pipe and the water continues to drip while you are trying to solder it, plug the dripping pipe with bread. Push the bread up beyond the joint. When the joint is repaired and the water turned back on, the bread will dissolve.

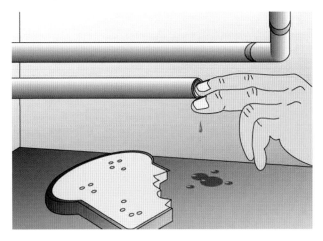

dowels, crosscutting

The problem with crosscutting dowels on a band saw is that they have a tendency to roll with the downward motion of the saw blade. Because of this, it is difficult to get a square crosscut even if you are holding it against the fence. Use the following technique: Make a V-shaped block and screw it to a strip of hardwood that will fit snugly into the tool's miter gauge groove. Extend the block about two inches beyond the blade. I used a piece of thick Plexiglas for the miter bar, because I had some scrap pieces lying around that just happened to fit. If everything is square, you'll get perfect cuts every time.

dowels, rounding over

Some woodworking processes require you to round over dowel ends. If the dowels required are in sizes that will fit into your drill/driver's chuck, set your drill in reverse and round over the dowel ends on a belt sander. The drill should rotate against the rotation of the sander.

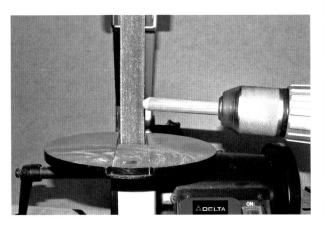

dowels, fluting

You may have been in a situation when you're about to glue up your project. The holes are drilled for the dowels, and you realize that you have no fluted dowels. If this is the case simply take ordinary doweling approximately a foot long, find a box wrench that is $\frac{1}{32}$" or $\frac{1}{16}$" smaller than the dowel, and, using a wooden mallet, tap the dowel through the wrench. You have a fluted dowel ready to be cut to size and used. If you have a pencil sharpener and the dowel will fit into it, slightly sharpen one end. This will make it easier to put it in the hole.

dowels, rounding over

Dowel ends can also be rounded over by inserting them in the chuck of a drill press. With the drill press turned on, use a power sander to chamfer them.

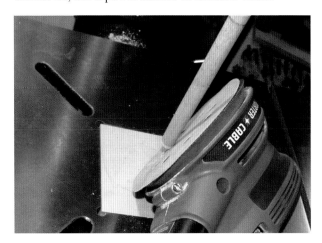

dowels, shop made

Don't throw away those foam paint brushes. Cut the handles off to be used as dowels at a later date as required.

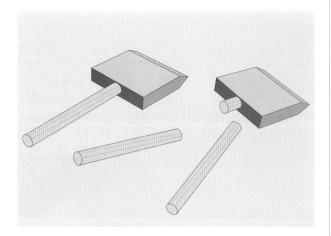

dowels, storing

Storing dowels, threaded rod and other similar items is made easy by visiting your local carpeting retailers. Ask them for a couple of the cardboard tubes used to roll the carpeting. I'm sure they would be happy to give you a few. With a hole saw or a fly cutter cut some scrap wood discs to fit in the ends. Screw the discs to a rectangular piece of scrap plywood and glue them to the discs. Cut the tubes long enough to store those items and place the unit in a convenient spot in your shop.

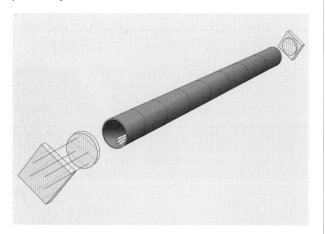

dowels, storing

Use ABS or PVC plastic pipe to store your dowels. Use whatever diameter you think you will need and then add an inch. Plumber's steel strapping can be used to mount the pipe on a wall.

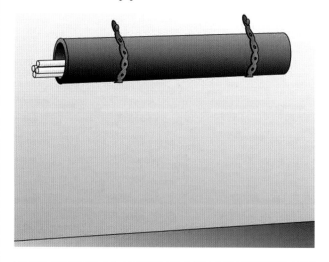

drywall mud, extend life

The "mud" used for joint-filling drywall (plasterboard) can dry out quickly. If you want to save the remaining mud for later use, level off the remaining amount in the container and then add some water. Add about two inches of it to cover the mud. Reseal the container and store it. When you plan to reuse it, simply pour off the water.

edge banding, homemade

Make your own edge banding on your table saw. Be sure to make the banding wider and longer than initially required so that it can be trimmed flush after application. This will provide a professional finish to your project.

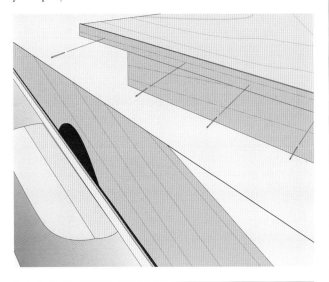

epoxy, mixing

Most people squeeze out a blob each of hardener and resin when making a batch of epoxy glue, to approximate a 50/50 mix. Not having the mix in the right proportions can result in weak glue and reduce its holding power. An easy solution to get a more accurate mixture is to squeeze a line out of the hardener and then a line of equal length from the resin. Now when you mix them, they will be of equal proportions. Some epoxy glue is packaged in a double hypodermic container to simplify this.

epoxy, mixing

A problem sometimes encountered when mixing epoxy hardener and resin is finding a clean, small suitable surface on which to mix them. One solution is to use the bottom of an unopened can of soda. It provides a shallow depression for easy mixing and is heavy enough so that it won't readily tip. Also, on hot days when epoxy tends to set up faster, you can cool the can in the refrigerator first. This will delay the hardening. One final note: When you have finished with the glue, don't set the can down on anything you might need. You might not be able to remove the can.

epoxy, retarding set-up

Epoxy glue will set up faster in warmer weather or in a warm environment. This may not be desirable in some situations. To retard this, mix your epoxy on top of a soda can, but refrigerate the can first. Another approach is to mix the glue on the lid of a jug filled with ice water.

extension cords, selecting

Care should be taken when using an extension cord for your portable or stationary power tools. Check the ampere rating of the tool that you are using along with the length of the extension cord. Use the table below for the recommended extension cord gauge. Using a lighter gauge than recommended can damage your tool.

Amps	25' Cord	50' Cord	75' Cord	100' Cord
0-5	18 gauge	18 gauge	18 gauge	18 gauge
10	18 gauge	18 gauge	16 gauge	16 gauge
12	16 gauge	16 gauge	16 gauge	16 gauge
15	14 gauge	14 gauge	14 gauge	14 gauge
20	12 gauge	12 gauge	12 gauge	12 gauge

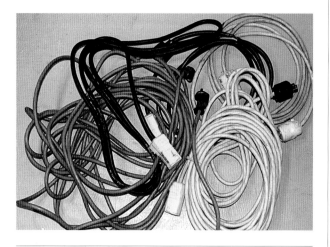

hardwood, board foot

Hardwood lumber is frequently sold by the board foot (a 1"-thick × 12"-wide × 12"-long piece of wood equals one board foot). To determine the quantity of board feet in a piece of hardwood: Thickness × width × length, divided by 144 (144 inches in a board foot).

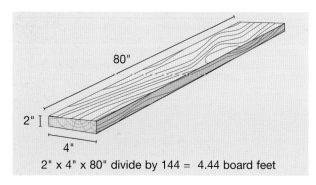

2" x 4" x 80" divide by 144 = 4.44 board feet

foam, cutting

Cutting rigid types of foam, such as Styrofoam, or the types of rubber foam that you find in chair seats, can be done easily on a band saw. Most types of band-saw blades will work with the exception of a skip-tooth blade, which will give a rougher cut. The best blades to use are the ones with the most teeth per inch. And, of course, the tighter the scroll pattern, the narrower the blade that is used. Freezing the rubbery type of foam overnight will make for a cleaner cut. Another method is to use an electric carving knife, if used on larger radii patterns and straight cuts. The ideal way of cutting foam is with a hot wire. This is the way professionals do it, but the setup is specialized.

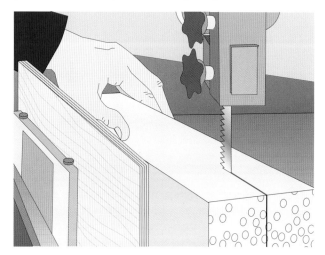

lumber, air drying

Never use air-dried lumber for interior furniture projects unless you have acclimatized the wood to your shop. Air-dried wood is usually considered dry at 14 – 17 % moisture content (MC), much too wet for interior cabinetry. Allow the wood to dry in an area that is similar in temperature and relative humidity as the final placement of the furniture. This is generally in the 7 - 8% MC range.

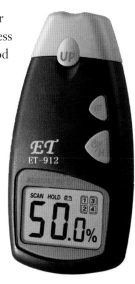

lumber, safe handling

Newly resawed or freshly planed boards should never be stored flat. This will allow the moisture to drain too quickly and the boards are sure to warp. Stand the boards on end to allow air to circulate around them but not on too sharp of an angle.

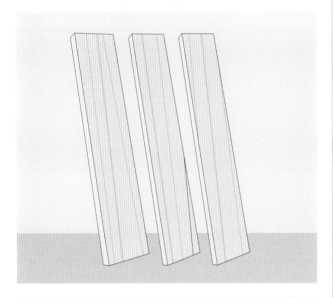

masking tape, extending life

The adhesive on masking tape sometimes dries out and just seems to tear off when you are looking for a long strip of it. Don't despair; put the roll in your microwave oven for about 15 seconds. This will soften the adhesive and make it stick once more.

lumber, storing

Storing lumber stacked in a rack where only the ends or the edges of the lumber are visible can make it difficult to determine what species of wood it is and how long it is. Here is a simple solution: First, use colored plastic tape to identify the type of wood, (yellow for oak, blue for pine). Your local hardware store sells plastic tape in packages of five or six colors. Staple the tape to the board ends. Second, to determine the length of each piece, write its length on the end of the board with a dark pencil or a felt marker. If you end up cutting a piece off a board, revise the dimension.

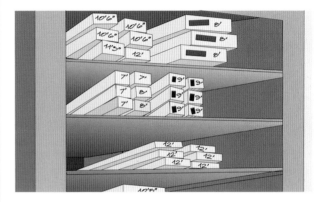

paraffin wax

Keep a block or two of paraffin wax in your shop. Paraffin is a great lubricant for adjustment screws like those on a jointer or to make it easier when screwing into hardwood species like oak. Paraffin also works really well on those sliding dovetails in drawers. Melt paraffin wax in a double boiler and use the liquid (careful it's hot) as food safe finish on salad bowls, cutting boards and the like.

plywood, adding edging

Here is a way to add edging to plywood. Let's assume, for example, that you want to add edging to a bookcase top that is 12" × 36". Cut your piece 12¼" × 36¼" to compensate for a ⅛" saw kerf. Now, using a radial arm saw, set your blade at a 45° angle and rip your top full length, making sure that you are cutting the full thickness. Do the same thing to the ends. Save the cut-offs. Turn them over and glue them back on in their respective positions. You now have veneered edges on four sides. A little practice on some scrap pieces will help.

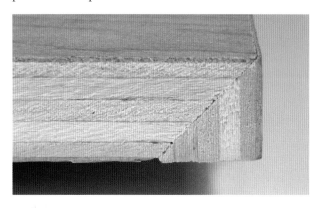

plywood, conservation

Plywood is expensive so you really don't want to waste any when building your next project. There are many free programs available on the internet, one of which is at www.maxcut.co.za. Or, you can do it manually by using a cross section pad with ¼" squares. Simply use the squares as a scale such as ¼" = 1' 0" to make the best use of a sheet.

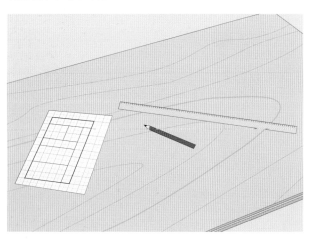

plywood, bending

Bending plywood, to use as edging for a round table for example, can be done easily, even with 3" thick material. Cut the piece to the desired length and width, being sure that the surface grain runs lengthwise on the strip. On the reverse side of the outer surface, start making crosscuts with your table saw, radial arm saw or compound miter saw. Make the cuts down to the outer surface ply and make them about a ½" apart. This distance will have to be by trial and error and will depend on the thickness of the plywood and the radius of the bend.

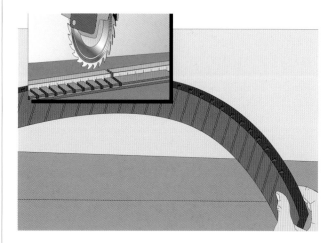

rust, preventing

Graham's law: Tools will rust. Unused tools will rust faster. Well, it's not really my law; Mother Nature enacted it long before I did. One way to sidestep this law is to get friendly with your neighborhood electronics dealers; the ones who sell televisions and stereos. Ask them to save the little packs of "silica gel" that are usually packed with the new equipment that they receive. Throw a couple of these in each of your tool chest drawers. They will absorb a lot of the moisture that causes your tools to rust.

rust, preventing

Rust Check is a rust-inhibiting, oil-like substance that is usually used on automobiles, but works equally well on tools. There is usually a Rust Check dealer in every town and city, so obtaining the product will not pose a problem. Somewhere in your workshop is a container full of rusty nuts, bolts, screws, and probably a screwdriver or two as well. Now's your chance to make use of them. Take an old windshield-washer fluid container and cut a rectangular piece out of one side. Leave the cap on. Dump the rusted parts in it and then pour either paint thinner or engine cleaner on them. Let them sit for a couple of days; then drain the paint thinner or engine cleaner and wipe the parts. Dry them off, clean out the container, put the parts back in, and spray Rust Check over them. After a day or so, drain but don't discard the Rust Check. The used Rust Check can be used again for a few more applications. Use Rust Check on such things as band-

saw table or circular-saw tables, hand plane and planer bases, or any other metal surface that may have a tendency to rust. Simply wipe it on generously, let it sit overnight, and then wipe it off. Spills can be cleaned up with dish detergent and water.

rust, preventing

Another way to prevent your tools from rusting is to spray silicone on the drawer bottoms of your tool chest. Do not do this with the tools in place. Spraying the tools will also prevent rust, but it will also make the handles and grips dangerously slippery. Make sure that the silicone has dried before placing the tools back in the drawers. Before using the tools, check the handles to make sure that there are no traces of the silicone on them. Any residue may be removed with mineral spirits.

rust, preventing

To help keep the tools in your tool cabinet rust-free, open the top of a box of baking soda and place it on one of the shelves. Baking soda is great for absorbing moisture in the air.

sawdust, safety

Sawdust is hazardous to your health! In addition to the fact that some species of wood can be toxic, a sawdust-filled workshop can be highly flammable. Dust that is floating in the air can be easily ignited by a spark or a flame. Do not smoke or allow any open flames in your workshop. Leaving sawdust on

the shop floor is like putting powdered wax on a dance floor. It makes it very slippery. A fall on a dance floor is embarrassing. A fall on your shop floor could be fatal. I vacuum my workshop at least once a week and I recommend you do the same.

screws, brass installing

Brass screws are really quite soft and will break easily by comparison but they really look nice in hardwoods like oak and walnut. To prevent the brass screws from breaking install a steel screw of the same size first. Remove it and then install the brass screw.

screws

Wood screws consist of a head and shank, with most or all of the shank being threaded. Wood screws come in a variety of different shapes. Each one is designed for a specific purpose. These shapes range from flat head to round head to pan head to bugle head. Most screws come in lengths starting at ¼" and go up to 6" or more. The diameter of the screw is called the gauge and is usually expressed in whole numbers, i.e., 7 × 1" long. The drive of the screw can vary as well, as can be seen in the photo below. The Robertson, or square-drive screw is very popular in Canada and the United States. This is my personal favorite because the drive will take more torque than a slot drive. Another advantage is that a Robertson screwdriver will hold the screw so that you can reach those difficult corners. The Quadrex screw will accept a Robertson and a Phillips screwdriver. The slot-drive screw is becoming obsolete. The bugle-head screw (also known as a drywall screw) is now regularly used in woodworking, especially for fastening plywood and other softwoods. These screws are often available in the Phillips drive, but I have seen them in square drives as well. The advantage is that they do not require a pilot hole. When using them, though, make sure that the two pieces of stock are held tightly before screwing, because there is no unthreaded shank to pull the pieces together. Another advantage is that the drywall screw is self-countersinking.

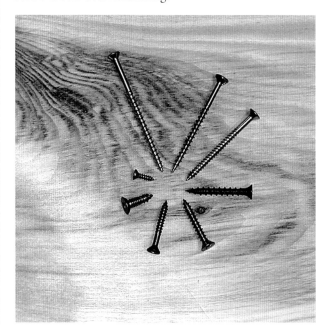

screws, broken

When a screw breaks off just as you are assembling your completed project, you count to ten, curse anyway, and then take your portable drill and carefully drill a $\frac{1}{16}$" hole on an angle through the edge of the wood and into the screw. Do this a couple of more times in different positions. Now, use a pair of needle-nose pliers to grip and remove the screw remains. The next step is to repair the hole. Drill a hole slightly larger than the existing one by using a bit that is equal in size to a dowel that you have on hand. Cut the dowel to its proper length and glue and insert it into the hole, making sure that the grain in the dowel runs in the same direction as your work piece. Select a screw larger in gauge than the one removed, drill a new pilot hole, and countersink and carefully drive the screw home.

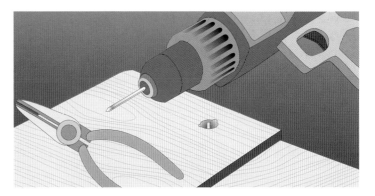

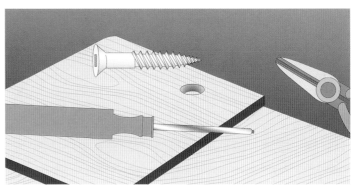

screws, countersink

To countersink for a screw that has to be placed in tight quarters, use a common nail. Hammer its head until it forms a U-shape. Put the nail through the screw hole, tighten it in the chuck of your portable electric drill and then pull it toward you until the desired depth is attained.

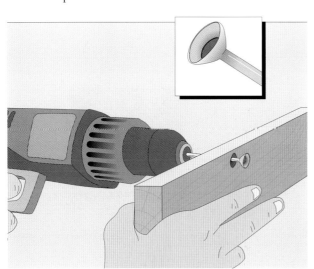

screws, countersink cover

Try this technique for making countersink covers: Buy a common paper-hole punch from a stationary store. This tool is great for punching out "dots" in veneer. Put a little contact cement on the screw head and the veneer and you have a perfect screw cover.

screws covers

Cabinetry screws can be ugly or attractive depending on what the woodworker envisions for the cabinet's final appearance. Some commercial woodworkers place rounded "buttons" on top of the recessed screws to both hide the screws and accent the connection. Some use fancy screws to accent the connection, and others use wood filler to hide the screws. Here are a couple of ways to completely camouflage them. Edge-banding veneer is available in most common wood types, and it usually has hotmelt-glue backing. If you are using a No.4 or No.5 screw, you can "punch" out circles with a standard office hole punch. Using an edge veneer that matches your project, place these circles over the recessed screws; they will virtually disappear. A heat gun will keep the circles in place. For larger screws, you can use a standard plug cutter to make the circles. This way, the circles can be made from a scrap piece that matches your work piece and then sliced off with a fine-toothed saw to fit. Although a plug cutter can be used in a portable drill, it is best to use a drill press because it will give a cleaner circle.

screw plugs

When making screw plugs in a piece of scrap with a plug cutter do not try to pry them out with a screwdriver as this will damage the edges of the plugs. Next time, do a whole series of plugs with your plug cutter and then run the scrap piece through your band saw.

screws, purchasing

The next time you are in your local hardware store to pick up some screws for your project, buy square-drive screws, also known as Robertson screws. These screws have a square hole in their tops and will take more torque than the conventional slot-or Phillips head screws. Another advantage is that the screwdriver will actually hold the screw so it can be placed in horizontal or overhead positions. These screws cost about the same as the other types of screws.

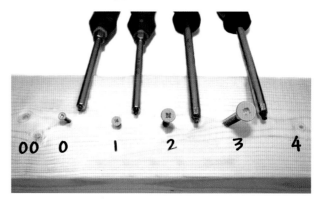

screws, selecting

Do not use the common steel screw when building projects out of oak and some other hardwoods. Over a period of time, the metal will react with the natural acids of the wood and black rings will appear around the screw holes. Select stainless steel or brass screws when working with oak. The screws are more expensive but they are worth it.

softwood, drying checks

When air-or kiln-drying softwood lumber, there is a tendency for the ends of the boards to check (split). To help deter this, a couple coats of an exterior latex paint on the board's ends may do the trick.

softwood, buying

Most lumberyards sell their softwood by the board foot, but some retail it by the running foot. Make sure you know which method before you buy. Never purchase lumber over the telephone; it is best to hand-pick the lumber to avoid defects that could affect your project. Look for boards that are straight and true. Look for knots that are loose or for checks (splits) in the ends of boards and avoid these. Boards that are cupped, twisted or warped should be avoided as well. Home woodworkers have a tendency to buy clear pine when in fact they can spend a lot less on knotty pine. First-grade knotty pine will have tight knots; simply coating the knots with shellac will prevent "bleed-through" into a painted finish. If you own a thickness planer, you will save money by purchasing rough lumber and dressing it yourself. For interior projects, never buy lumber on the same day that you plan to use it. Wood has to acclimate to its surroundings for several days or more, depending on the moisture content. Most lumberyards will have a moisture meter on hand for you to use. Lumber will shrink as it dries and, if wet, it should be stored flat in a warm, dry area and have stickers (equal-sized strips of wood placed every two or three feet) between the boards to allow air to circulate.

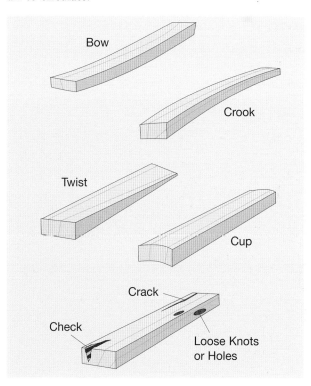

solvents, disposing of

It's so easy to go into your local paint or hardware store, order a gallon or so of paint thinner or the like, use it, and then dump the used material down the drain. Right? Wrong! Please do not do that. Pour the waste into an empty plastic container, save it until it is full (store it outside), and then bring it to your local environmental waste disposal depot and ask them to dispose of it. This applies not only to solvents, but to paint, lacquer, varnish, contact cement, thinner, wood filler, paint remover, or any other product that is labeled toxic or hazardous. I don't want to get on my soapbox here, but I do want to point out that as responsible woodworkers the only assurance that we and our children have to continue in our business or hobby is to look after our environment. Sounds trite? Maybe so, but let's continue our enjoyment of woodworking, and let's make sure that there are enough healthy trees to do so. Now, here are a couple of techniques to temporarily dispose of some of those hazardous materials. Pour your used material in a

container of cat litter. Let it dry. When you have a sufficient quantity, call or take it to the disposal depot for safe disposition. Another solution is to "paint" the material on the walls of an old barn or shed and let the sun dispose of it. Probably, however, the best solution is to give consideration to the "environmentally friendly" materials that are safe and water-soluble.

tape, backing leader

Double-faced tape has a lot of uses around the shop, but if you just tear a length of it off the roll, separating the tape from the backing strip can be a problem. Next time that you need a length of it, peel the tape off of the backing first and then tear off only the tape portion. Leave a "leader" of the backing in place. By making this a routine, future strips will tear off easily.

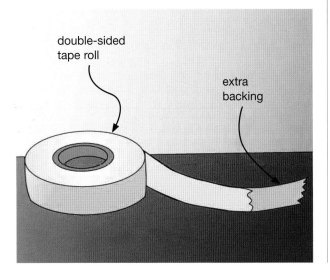

double-sided tape roll

extra backing

tape, double-faced

Double-faced tape can prove to be an invaluable tool in the workshop. The tape comes in many forms, but cloth, paper or the no-substrate types are best. The paper type is best used in pattern duplication where you want to stack several thin pieces together and make only one cut, say, on a scroll saw. The tape without any substrate can be used here as well. Cloth tape such as that used for carpeting can be used for thicker stock duplication. When using double-faced tape for project duplication, it is important not to adhere any over a cut line. The tape will bind to the saw blade and will make cutting difficult.

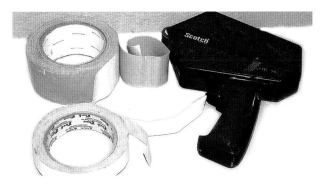

tape, removing

Sticky tape and price labels can be a real pain to remove and for some unknown reason, retailers and manufacturers always seem to place them where they shouldn't be. WD-40 to the rescue! Once you get the paper or plastic part of the labels off, a couple of squirts of this product will either melt or dissolve the adhesive. Be sure to wipe it all clean though.

veneer, repairing blisters

Repairing a blister in veneer, use a snap-off blade knife to slit the blister down the middle of it. Raise the edge of the cut and use a small spatula to force wood glue into the opening. Squeeze as much glue out of the blister as you can and then clamp a board wrapped in saran wrap over the blister to close it until the glue sets.

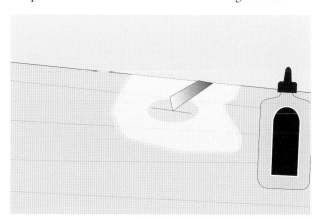

veneer, making

Make your own veneer for smaller projects on your band saw using a shop-made point fence. The illustration shows how the point fence is made.

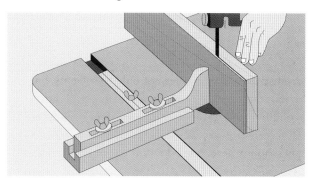

veneer, repairing blisters

Occasionally a bubble will appear on a piece that you have recently veneered. Most likely, this is due to an absence of glue beneath that spot, Or the glue in that spot was too dry to adhere. If the latter is true, apply some heat to the area with a hair dryer or heat gun. Be careful not to burn it; get it just hot enough so that you can still touch it. Now, place a heavy weight on top of the area to compress the bubble onto the heated surface. Let it stand for a few hours. If this doesn't work, it's because there was no glue to adhere to, so try the following technique: Check online to find source for syringes. They usually come with a large-gauge, blunt-tipped needle. Get one that is large enough to allow woodworking glue to pass through with some pressure. Put a few drops of the glue into the syringe and inject it into the bubble. Clamp the spot down. The bubble will disappear. Rinse the syringe out thoroughly in warm water, replace the safety cap, and lock it away for future use.

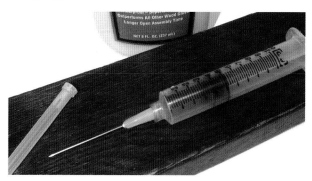

veneer, repairing edges

Sometimes the veneered edges of workpieces get lifted and break away. This is usually due to poor glue adhesion at the outset. Should this happen, use a sharp knife like a snap-off blade tool to cut a rectangular shape of the missing veneer. Clean the area of old glue residue and then try to match the veneer of the missing portion. Cut it to size and using contact cement, glue it back on.

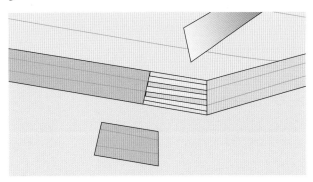

wood, storing

There is a right and a wrong way to air-dry lumber or hardwood. The wrong way is to haphazardly stack the wood in the lumber rack. This will usually result in warped, twisted, or crooked material. Try this technique to store lumber properly. Next time you are out making a purchase at your favorite lumberyard, buy a bundle of laths. When your lumber arrives, layout three laths (assuming that they are 4' long) and place a layer of lumber perpendicular on top of them. Place three more laths on top of the first layer, etc. There should be a lath in the middle and one about a foot from each end. Use more than three laths if your stock is longer than 8' long. Now, the important part! The laths should all be in the same position; that is, if you are looking at a stack of lumber, the laths should form a straight vertical line. If the laths are not straight up and down, the result may be kinks in the boards. Also make sure that the annual rings on the lumber arch upward. It will allow moisture to drain down, rather than form a pocket that will result in a cup. The reason, of course, for doing any of the above is to ensure free air circulation while acclimatizing the material and to further ensure that your material stays straight and true.

wood filler, applying

Most woodworkers are familiar with the application of the various types of wood filler. We all have little accidents or mistakes that we want to hide. To make that joint look perfectly mitered, we fill in the cracks with wood filler. The toughest mistakes to fix on the surface are dings or dents made by a hammer. It seems that wood filler just won't stay put, no matter what you do. Here's the answer: Use your electric drill with a $\frac{1}{16}$" bit and drill a couple of shallow holes in the dent. These holes will allow the wood filler to grab onto something.

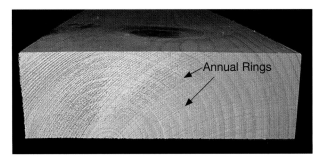

Annual Rings

wood, transporting

Protect your car's rooftop luggage rack when you visit your home renovation center to pick up a load of lumber. Use a couple of foam water-pipe insulation tubes and wrap them around the crossbars first.

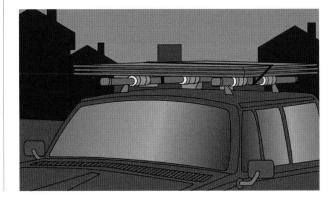

MATH

angles, drawing

No protractor? No problem. Use your table saw's miter gauge. Line up the gauge with the edge of the board that you want the angle drawn on. Set the angle and then simply flip the gauge over to mark the line. *Tip: If you want your angle sloped to the left, set the miter gauge to the right. When you flip it, the angle will be correct.*

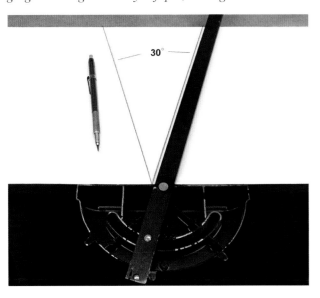

angles, drawing

Let's suppose that you have to draw a 22.5-degree line across the face of a 2" × 12" board. Here is a simple solution using the angle jigs shown. You place the jig against the edge of the work piece and draw a line. Use a straight-edge to complete the line across the full width of the board if the board is wider than the jig.

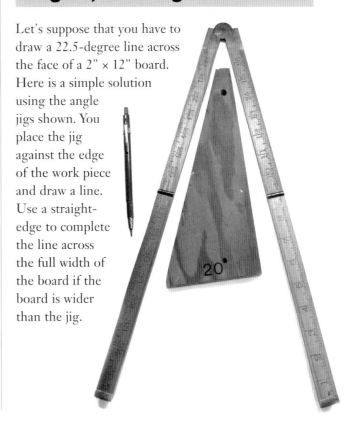

angles, finding centers

Here is a technique for finding the centers of angles. When cutting out triangles, hexagonals, octagorials, etc., don't throwaway the cut-offs. For example, if you want to drill a hole in the middle of a triangular piece of wood, use double-faced or masking tape to reattach a cut-off to one or more sides of the triangle. (I use a piece of ⅛-inch Plexiglas to fill in the saw kerf, and then tape the pieces together.) When you are using a square, one side will be "true." Now, draw a line vertically across the piece. Move the cut-off to another side of the triangular piece and repeat the process. Now repeat this process one more time and you will end up with converging lines. Where they converge is the center point, as shown.

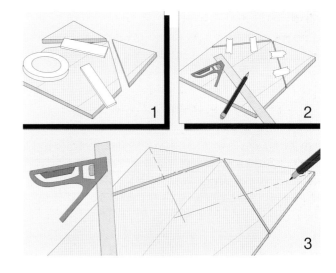

angle jigs

Precise angles, such as 7½-degrees, are sometimes difficult to set on various tools such as compound miter saws, radial arm saws, etc. Making a set of angle jigs out of ¾" plywood and keeping them handy will save a lot of work and calculations later. These jigs can be used with a drill press, belt sander, table saw, band saw and even some portable tools.

center finding jig

As an example, let's assume that you want to work on a piece of stock that is 5¹³⁄₁₆" wide and you have to find the center of it. One way to do this is to cut a 10" length of ¾" stock. Make a mark exactly 1" from each end and in the exact center of the stock. With your drill press, drill ¼" inch holes into the marks at both ends. Glue a ¼"-diameter × 1¼"-long dowel into each end. Check the diameter of the pencil that you usually use and drill a hole for it precisely into the center of the stock. Now, simply place your pencil in the hole, slide the jig down the stock, and you have a centerline.

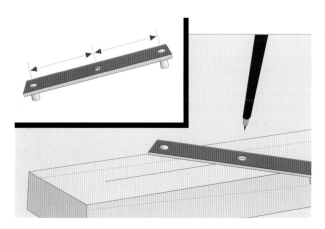

centers, drawing

The next time you use a compass to draw a circle on wood or plastics and you don't want to see that hole in the middle that a compass usually makes, this technique will help. First, find your approximate center. Next, lay two or three layered strips of masking tape across the work piece to form an X. Measure to find your exact center and use the masking tape to support your compass point. Because plastics scratch so easily, you may want to put five or six layers of tape down.

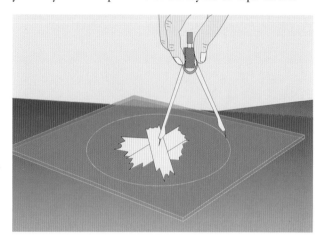

center finding jig

Another method for finding the centers of stock. Let's assume that you have a board that is 10⅜" wide and you want to find its center. Take your builder's square, place the bottom corner of the long side at one edge of the stock, and move it up on an angle until the other edge of the stock joins a whole number, i.e., 8". Now simply divide the whole number by two.

chalk line, uses

Most people think of a chalk line as a tool that should only be in a house-builder's toolbox. Not so. The chalk line can be used for a multitude of things in the home workshop. For example, the chalk line is a

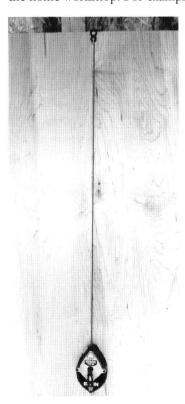

quick and easy way to make a line for ripping a 4×8 sheet of plywood. It will also make a clear vertical line for nailing in those first and subsequent studs against a foundation wall, and can be used on the end gables of a bookcase to give you a straight line for screwing in shelves. You don't have a plumb bob? The chalk line works just as well. And the list goes on.

chalk line, using correctly

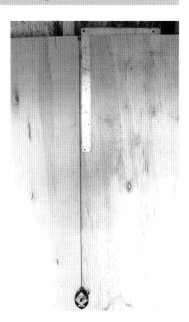

Use the chalk line correctly, though. First, make sure that your measurement is accurate, and then set the hook of the line precisely so that the chalked line is on your measurement mark. Use a steel square to true the line and then pull it taut and hold it at the reel end. Now, grasp the middle of the line and pull straight up. Let go and the line will snap down and leave a definitive and straight chalk mark on your workpiece. The important point to remember is to pull the cord straight up or the resulting line will be distorted. A rainbow of powdered chalk is available so that the line will stand out on a wide range of materials. I prefer blue, as it seems to have an iridescent glow that makes it visible on almost any material. A damp cloth will wipe away any traces of the line.

circles, drawing

There will be times when you will want to draw circles and do not have a circle compass available. Here's a simple method for drawing circles up to 24" without one. Let's assume that you want to draw a circle with an 8" radius. With your builder's square, draw a straight line across your stock. Then drive two small nails along the line, 8" apart. Lay your builder's square flat on the stock, with the inside corner around the first nail. Put your pencil at the 8" mark of the square and simply rotate the square and your pencil up and around until the square hits the center nail. This will produce an arc. Flip the square and repeat for the next half.

circles, patterns

This technique will save you a great deal of time in the future when you want to make circles for wheels, etc. Cut a 12"-diameter piece of ¹⁄₁₆"-thick polystyrene and find and mark its center. Draw a line completely up the center. Mark the line exactly every 1" from the center to one outer edge. On the other half of that line make a mark every 1", skipping the whole numbers. Start at the ½" mark, (½", 1½", 2½", etc.). Now, draw an intersecting line completely across the circle. Mark it every ½". Begin at ¼" and skip the ½" and the whole numbers (¼", ¾", 1¼", 1¾", etc.). On the right side, make a mark every ¼". Begin at the ⅛", eliminating the ¼" and ½" marks and the whole numbers. Drill a ¹⁄₁₆" hole at each of these marks, including the center. Drill a ¼" hole in a blank area near the top for hanging, sand off the burrs on the back, and, with a fine felt-tip marker, mark the names of the lines. Finally, use a compass to draw a circle only at the inch

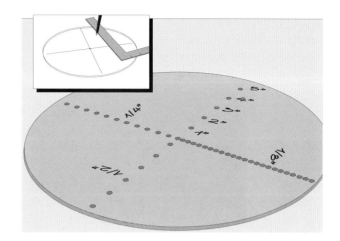

line holes. To use this device, place it on your work piece, tap in a finishing nail in the center, put a pencil point in the desired hole and rotate it. The whole numbers on the jig shown represent the radii, not the diameters.

compass, using

The compass I'm referring to here is the architect's or draftsman's compass that is used to make circles. Mind you, I've seen people go around in circles using a magnetic one. However, the circle compass has been used and abused for eons now and this astounds me. The usual type of compass will accurately draw a radius of about three inches. This is accomplished with both arms of the compass at about 15 degrees off the vertical. I have seen woodworkers stretch this to 45 and 60 degrees and expect to get a perfect circle. They are really surprised to see that the finish line does not meet the start line. Some compasses are called "free arm" because they can be opened up until they are almost flat.

compass, using

Other types have a screw mechanism that restricts the opening to allow for an accurate circle. The free-arm types sometimes have "elbows" in them to allow for accurate stretched circles, while the ones with the screw gears accept extension arms (beams) to stretch their reach. To draw an accurate circle, make sure the lead pencil point is sharp and that the pin is close to vertical. If it isn't, it has more of a chance to slip and perhaps make an eccentric circle.

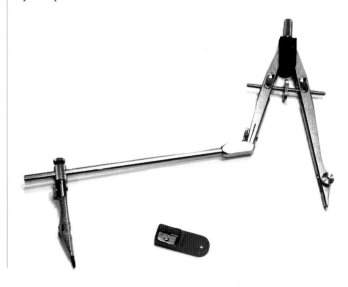

compass, shop made

Here is a technique for making a compass that will create circles up to 72" in diameter. Get hold of a wooden or aluminum yardstick. Drill holes precisely on the top of the 1" marks and at the same position on the width of the ruler cut a small notch on the ends. Tap a nail into the center of your project. With a ruler notched against the nail insert a pencil into the desired hole and rotate it.

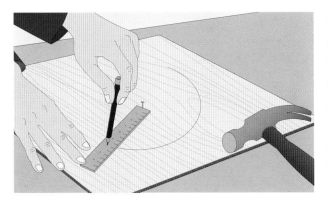

compass, shop made

If you happen to mislay your compass and you urgently have to draw a circle, try this: Use either a hacksaw blade or a reciprocal saw blade. A nail through the hole in the blade will hold it on its axis and the blade teeth should hold your pencil. It works!

curves, drawing

When laying out curves you can use a ⅛" thick × ¼" wide length of hardwood. A straight-grained species works best. Drill a ⅛" hole in each end and thread a cord through. Tie a knot in one end and on the other, use a cord lock. This is that spring loaded gismo that you find on windbreakers to tighten the waist or the hood. Pull on the cord to provide you with the desired arc.

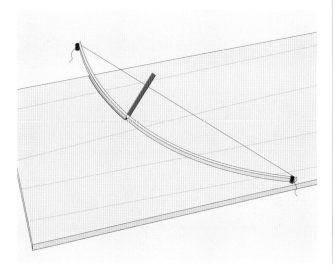

curves, duplicating

Freehand scalloping or decorative scroll work is great if you can make both halves of a piece of work the same. Let's assume, for example, you're making the scalloped back piece for an antique dresser. You have drawn half the pattern freehand and you have to duplicate it for the other half, but can't quite get it right. Do the following: Cut the first half on the band saw, cut the scrap off, flip the first-half piece over, and trace it on the other half of your stock. The pattern will be duplicated precisely.

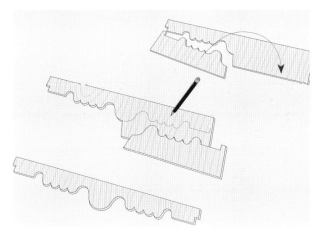

curves, making freehand

Making freehand curves for scalloped edges, etc. is now an easy task. A flexible curve is available at a reasonable price from most art supply dealers. The flexible curve is made of vinyl and has material inside that makes it flexible on the horizontal plane and allows it to retain its shape. Get the longest flexible curve (36") if you are making furniture. You'll find it really handy.

dowels, finding center

One simple way of finding the center of a dowel is to drill a hole the size of the dowel into a piece of scrap wood. Push the dowel partway into the hole and then, with a wooden mallet, tap a Forstner or brad-point bit into the other end of the hole. The drill bit should be the same size as the dowel.

dowels, finding center

Another easy way to find the center of a dowel is to use a center finder. This device has a blade set at 45 degrees that cuts a line into the end of a dowel. Hold the dowel tight in the corner, tap it with a hammer, rotate it 90 degrees, tap again, and you will have located its center. It can also be used for 2×2s or smaller pieces of wood. (Lines exaggerated for clarity)

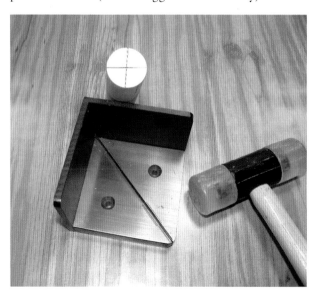

dowels, marking

To mark a straight circumference line on a dowel, table leg or even a turning, find the position where you want that line. Then wrap an index card or other piece of cardboard around the workpiece until the ends meet and are square. Use a pencil to trace a line.

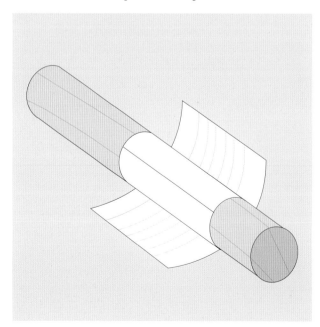

geometry

No, we are not going back to school. This is just a reference for some of the geometry terms that you may have forgotten and that you may find useful while working in your workshop. The illustration below left shows the various shapes of rectangles. Below right is shown the various shapes of triangles.

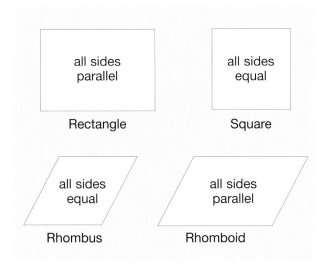

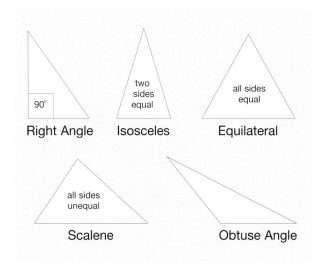

measuring, 1·2·3 blocks

Setting the depth, width and even the length of a cut can be extremely easy. A set of three shop-made wooden blocks called one-two-three blocks can be used alone or in various combinations to give accurate measurements from 1"- 9". The blocks, usually made of a kiln-dried hardwood, are made precisely 1" thick × 2" wide × 3" long. They must be square all around and their dimensions must be precise. One-two-three blocks (precision cut and made out of steel) have been used for years in the machining industry.

measuring, fractional blocks

When you have one-two-three blocks made of fractional plywood blocks, you have an almost infinite number of measuring possibilities without even touching your tape measure. Also, they are high enough to include any out-set teeth on a table saw, radial arm saw, or band-saw blade and thus will give an accurate measurement every time. One other benefit is that if your blocks are truly square, you can use them to determine the accuracy of your saw blades. Drill a hole in the blocks and hang them up close to your stationary power tools. Canadian and European readers should be aware that some plywood producers use the metric system in thicknessing plywood.

measuring, depth gauge

Those nylon tie wraps are just the thing for checking the depth of holes, mortises or to transfer a measurement. Cut off the locking end of the tie wrap. There are a variety of tie wrap sizes from very small to large.

measuring, story sticks

Professional cabinet makers often use story sticks for repeated projects. Make your story sticks do double duty. Some aluminum yardsticks are blank on the back. Use a pencil or non-permanent felt marker on this surface. The flip side of course is a ruler and a straight edge.

octagons

As defined by Webster's dictionary, an octagon is an eight-sided object with parallel sides that are equal. To make an octagonal chair or table leg, try using the following method: Take a piece of ¾" scrap and cut it just slightly longer than the width of your table leg. Drill and then insert dowels in the ends as shown. Divide the space between the dowels into thirds and drive two-inch finishing nails through the piece so that the points just protrude. You may want to use the drill press with a bit just slightly smaller than the nail. Hold the jig on your stock so that the dowels are firm against the sides and proceed to scribe down the length of the stock. Now you can plane or cut along the lines to make your leg.

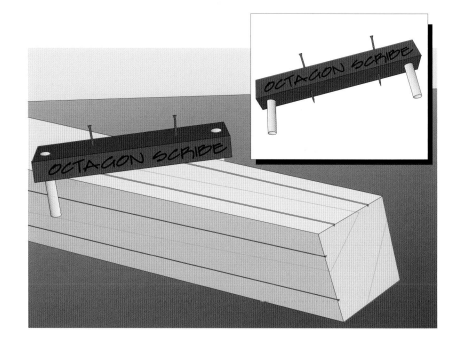

patterns, drawing

Drawing a pattern for cutting on pine, spruce or oak with a lead pencil makes it easy to see. Drawing a pattern on walnut or rosewood with the same pencil makes it difficult to see. To highlight that pencil line for better visibility, outline it with a yellow wax crayon that lumberyards use. This will make the line easier to follow and will not harm the wood.

patterns, full-size

Full size project design plans can be awkward to handle in most woodshops. For example, in my shop there is very little free bench-top space on which to spread out the plans. I've found the solution however. I've installed an inexpensive roll-down window shade in my shop and use masking tape to hold the plans in place; then roll them out of the way when I'm done.

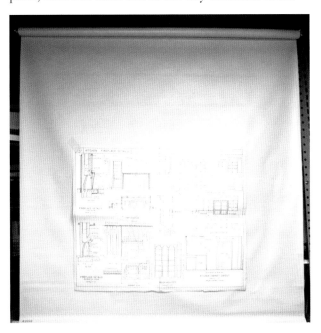

patterns, enlarging

A fender washer can be used to enlarge a wood pattern by say, a half inch all around. Fender washers are those large diameter washers with the small holes in them. Use a fender washer butted up against the pattern edge and a pencil in the hole and simply roll the washer around the pattern.

patterns, template removal

When applying a hardboard pattern or template to your workpiece with double faced tape, it is best to route a slight chamfer on an edge of the template. By doing this you will make it easier to get a chisel under the pattern to remove it without damage.

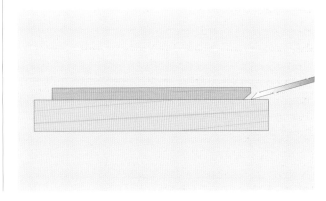

patterns, transferring

One way to transfer a pattern to the workpiece is to cut it with a utility knife and scissors and then trace it on the work piece using a sharp pencil.

patterns, transferring

Instead of transferring patterns from a project book onto paper or even directly onto your workpiece, buy a couple of sheets of white polystyrene from your local plastics dealer, They come in various thicknesses (gauges), so buy a thickness that can be easily cut with a pair of scissors or a utility knife. Now, photocopy your pattern and stick it onto the polystyrene with double-faced tape Or rubber cement. Then cut it out with a utility knife. Lightly sand the rough spots off the edges with very fine sandpaper. Adhere the pattern to your work piece with double-faced tape and trace around it with a sharp pencil. When you are done, write a description of the pattern on the pattern itself with a soft-tip marker, drill a hole in the pattern, and hang it up for future use.

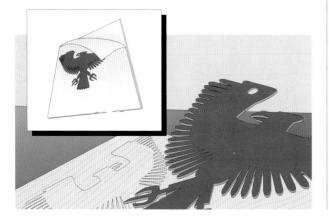

patterns, transferring

Transferring the patterns from the pattern book to your work piece can be a tedious operation. The usual method consists of dividing the pattern into, for example, ½" squares and then doing the same on your stock. To double the pattern size, you use 1" squares on the stock. Now there is an easy way: Photocopying. You simply make a high-contrast photocopy of the pattern, reducing or enlarging as required. Most libraries, post offices and drugstores have coin operated machines available. Once the photocopy is done, place it upside-down on the work piece and, using an iron that is not too hot, press it onto the wood.

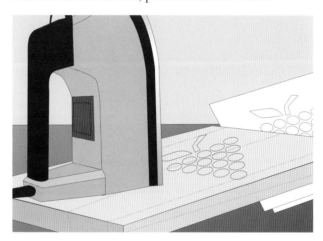

polygons, calculating

To determine the bevel angle for cutting a polygon or a column with a number of sides, divide 360 degrees by the number of sides you want the column to have and then divide that number in half. For example, to cut an eight-sided (octagon) column, divide 360 by 8 = 45 degrees. Divide that by 2 = 12½. So you would set your table saw blade to 12½ degrees.

polygons, types

By definition, a polygon is a geometric figure having three or more equal sides. Most of these shapes have names. Here they are:

Triangle:
Square:
Pentagon
Hexagon
Heptagon
Octagon:
Nonagon:
Decagon:
Undecagon:
Dodecagon:

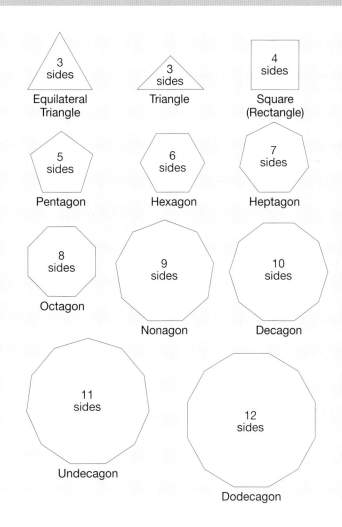

pulleys, sizing

Sizing pulleys has always been a trial-and-error situation for most woodworkers. The math grads probably find it a snap. For the rest of us, this may help. Let's suppose you want to build your own bench grinder. You have an electric motor and the speed is marked on it in rpm (rotations per minute, for example, 1,725). The grinder has a 2½" pulley already on its shaft. You want to increase the speed of the grinding wheel to around 4,000 rpm. What size should the pulley be on the motor shaft? The formula is easy with a calculator. Multiply 4,000 by 2½ and then divide by 1.725. You end up with a calculation of 5.797. This is the diameter of the pulley required to attain the desired speed. A 6" pulley will do just fine.

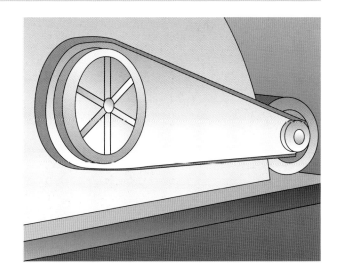

SHOP HELPERS

drilling, depth stop

Neoprene tubing is inexpensive and a couple of inches of it makes for a great depth stop for either your portable drill or even your drill press. Cut the right diameter tube to length and slide it on your drill bit.

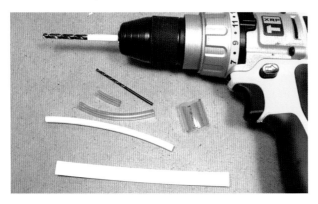

drilling, depth stop

Most portable ½" electric drills are equipped with a side handle that just screws into position. Some ⅜" drills have them as well, or at least the holes are there to accommodate one. If you are hand-drilling holes where the depth of the hole is critical, the depth stop shown here might work for you. Simply cut a length of perforated steel strapping and install it between the side handle and the drill housing. Measure the strapping for the depth of cut with the appropriate bit in the chuck and cut it off with tin snips. If your drill does not have a threaded hole for a handle, use a nylon tie wrap, cord or piece of elastic to secure the strapping.

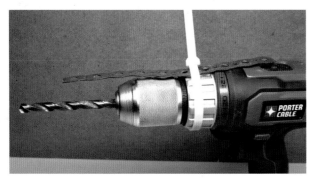

drilling, depth stops

When using your portable drill to make repeated holes that must be a specific depth, this shop-made jig will help. Use a piece of 1" × 1" hardwood. Cut it to the length of the drill bit that you plan to use. Using that same drill bit, bore down through the center of the 1×1. Hold the jig on the drill to determine the depth you want and cut the 1×1 accordingly.

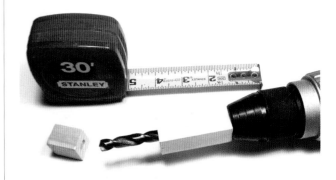

extension cord, storing

Don't get tripped up in extension cords. There is little that is more dangerous than having extension cords strewn on the shop floor. They can be invisible when buried under sawdust. Use a few hooks screwed into the ceiling so that they hang overhead and are less dangerous. Use a bungee cord to hold the plug close to the ceiling when not in use.

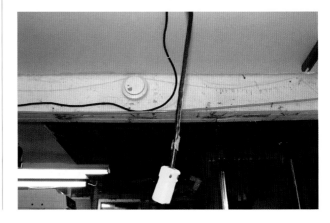

extension cord, storing

Keeping your extension cords in order is easier if you use those hook and loop ties. These have the hook on one side and the loop on the other, simply coil your extension cords and keep them that way with the ties.

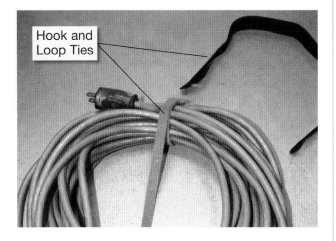

Hook and Loop Ties

extension cord, storing

Keep your power tool cords neatly wrapped by using hook and loop garden ties.

extension cord, storing

Most woodworkers have to rummage through a box or drawer to find that 50' or l00' extension cord. Once found, it takes a half-hour or so to disentangle it. There is an easy way to store extension cords so that they are readily accessible. Drill a hole in the side of a plastic pail, close to its bottom. Make the hole large enough for the plug end of the extension cord to just fit through. With the plug end sticking out of the hole, coil the rest of the cord into the bucket. Plug in the end from the hole into an outlet and simply reel out the amount of cord needed.

extension ladder, carrying

An extension ladder will be easier to carry if you hold it at the balance point. Hold the ladder near the center when not extended to find the center point. Finding that balance point later will be easier if you paint the spot with red paint.

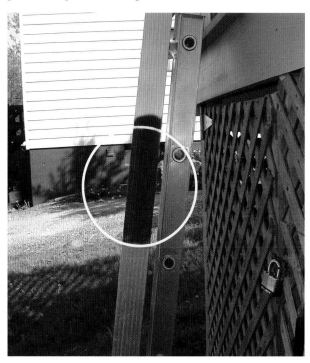

extension ladder, carrying

Foam pipe insulation wrapped at the balance point of your extension ladder will make hauling it around a little easier on your hands or shoulders.

extension ladder, paint can

Squeeze-type bar clamps can be used to hold a gallon of paint on an extension ladder while you are painting.

extension ladder, transport

Transporting an extension ladder on your car's roof rack can be made easier if you clamp it down with squeeze-type bar clamps.

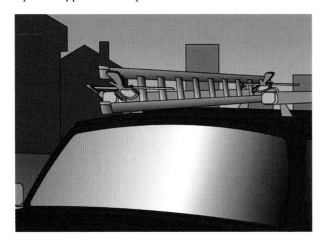

extension ladder, protection

Tape a few pieces of foam pipe insulation to the top of your extension ladder to protect the walls and siding of your house.

featherboards, making

Commercial featherboards may or may not suit your particular needs and making them in your shop is not a formidable job. Simply use a piece of ½" scrap wood that is 10" long and 4" or 5" wide. With your band saw make a full series of cuts spaced ⅛" apart and 4" long into the length of the board. When done, make a 30 degree cut across the end. Make several while you are at it.

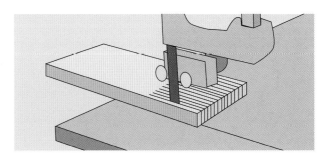

funnels, making

You can never find a funnel when you need one. Here's an easy and quick solution for making one. Simply cut the top off a two-liter plastic bottle of soda carefully on a band saw or by using a utility knife. Make the cut 3" to 4" below the top. While you're at it, cut several bottles and keep them near your paint. If you want to hang the funnels up, drill a hole in one side just below where you are going to cut the plastic bottle, and then cut the bottle. Don't throw away the caps on the soda bottles. The funnels make good mixing containers; the caps will seal the ends.

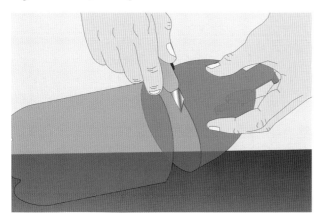

labels, removing

You've just bought a shiny new bench plane and you are ready to use it, but the price sticker you want to remove seems as if it's welded to the base plate. A simple way to remove it is to give it a couple of squirts of WD-40. Let the WD-40 soak for a few minutes, and then rub off the label and the WD-40 with a paper towel.

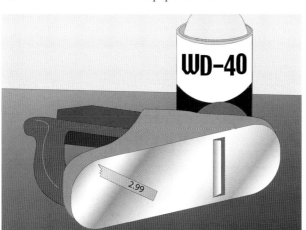

gluing racks

You can fit scrap pieces of 2×4 stock over your sawhorses to make a gluing rack. The slots on the bottom of the gluing rack should be cut so that they fit snugly on top of your sawhorse. The upper slots will hold your bar or pipe clamps, depending on the cut. The big advantage of this gluing rack is that it will not take up space on your workbench while you are waiting for glue to dry.

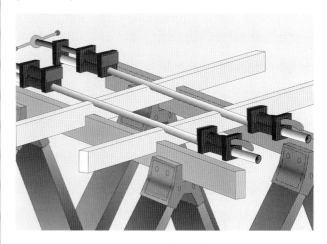

lamp, portable

To make a drafting lamp (the type with the spring arms) more portable use your hand screw clamp. Drill a hole on the top that is the same size as the lamp's post. Now you can move it almost anywhere in the shop.

83

lumber, storage rack

Build an inexpensive lumber rack with 4×4s and angle iron. Cut the angle iron in 2' lengths, drill a hole in the ends for lag screws. With a circular saw cut kerfs into the 4×4s at 2' intervals to fit one edge of the angle iron into. Screw the angle iron into the 4×4s. Securely fasten the 4×4s to a wall.

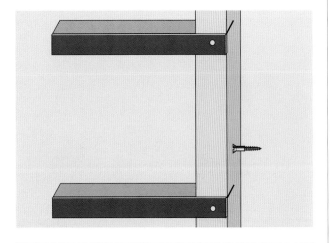

magnets

Magnets are real handy in the workshop; they will keep saw blade wrenches, router wrenches, drill press chuck keys and other accessories connected to the tool that they belong to. The best types to use are the rare earth magnets (made of neodymium iron boron), because they have the strongest pull. Using a steel washer between the magnet and the tool surface will increase the pull by a factor of four.

magnets

Another way to use magnets is to attach one (any type will do) to the end of a broom handle with epoxy glue. You can use this magnet to pick up those small screws, finishing nails and staples that drop on the floor. Next time you visit your local home improvement or electronics store, pick up a dozen or so of these magnets.

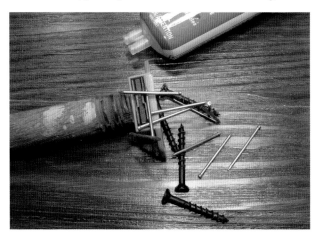

pegboard, cabinet doors

The insides of your shop cabinet doors are wasting space if you don't make use of them. Offset appropriately sized pegboard and attach to the insides of the doors and hang tools from them.

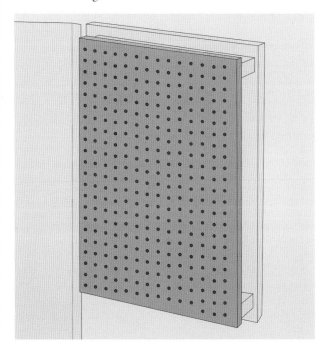

pegboard, securing hooks

One of the most annoying things about pegboard is the way that the hooks keep falling off when you remove a tool. A number of companies that make the hooks also make clips that go around the hooks and fasten into the holes. The problem is, I can never seem to find them in the store. Here's an easy and inexpensive way to solve the problem: Plug in your glue gun. When it's hot, squirt a little hot glue in the hole where you intend to put the hook. While the glue is still hot, install the hook. For longer hooks, repeat the above but also place some glue into a lower hole. Be sure that the glue goes into the hole and around the shaft of the hook.

pegboard, stationary tools

In addition to the obvious use on the wall for tool storage, pegboard has many more uses. Here's one. Most stationary power tools come equipped with an open sheet-metal stand. Try covering one, two or three sides of the stand with pegboard. It also makes a great place to hang saw blades, miter gauges and other tool related accessories. Don't stop there. Make a shelf out of pegboard that will fit on the stretchers that support the base. The pegboard's holes will let most of the sawdust run through, and the shelf will come in handy.

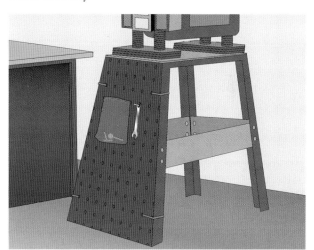

pegboard, tool identification

Now, using a black (or any color) soft-tip marker, trace around all the tools and other paraphernalia. There are stick-on labels available that silhouette just about every hand tool known to woodworkers. By doing this it will become obviously apparent if something is missing on the board.

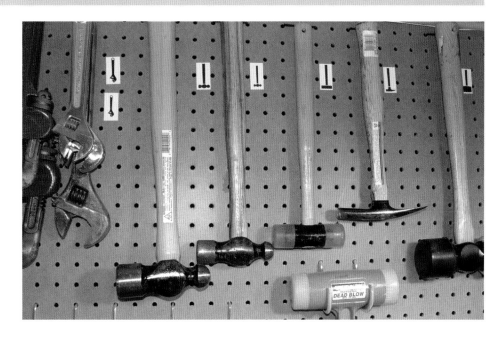

pegboard, tool identification

If your friends, neighbors and family members are quick to borrow tools but slow to return them, hang a little note on the hook of the borrowed tool to remind you who has it. If the paper starts to turn yellow, it's time to go looking for the tool.

pencils, drafting

The problem with carpenters' pencils, those round or flat, thick pencils that can leave a mark on virtually any material, is that they are too big, especially when you are marking fractional measurements. A regular lead pencil always breaks the minute you hit a knot or some cross-grain wood. A drafting mechanical pencil will prove much more helpful. These pencils are inexpensive and can be bought at an art-supply dealer. The advantage of this type of pencil is that if the lead breaks, you press the button for more. Also, the lead can be sharpened to a fine point. Buy one with the built-in lead point sharpener on the top. Also buy a package of "N2" leads. These leads are blacker, stronger and will stand out better than regular leads when you are making lines on darker woods.

pencils, keeping it handy

Some woodworkers that I know (including myself) have trouble remembering where they last put their shop pencil, but I've found the answer. I was at a meeting where they provided me with a name tag and a lavaliere to hang it from. Well, the meeting is over and I kept the lavaliere. Now, I hang my drafting pencil around my neck.

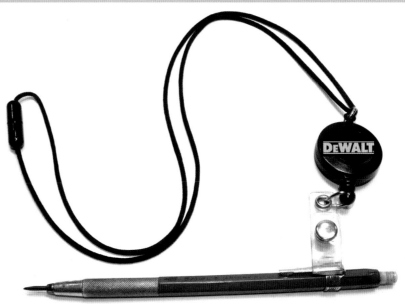

pencils, marking

Regular pencils are great for measurement marking on pine, basswood, poplar and other light colored wood species. However, marking lines on darker woods like rosewood, ebony, walnut and the like requires a trip to your art supply store. A white pencil or fine marker will do the trick nicely.

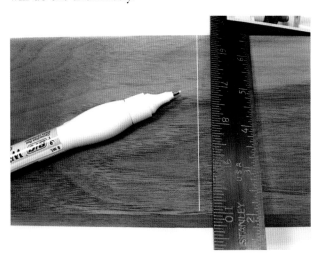

pencils, sharpening

Sharpening a shop pencil is usually done with a utility knife and that can be a hit-or-miss situation. Invariably when you get close to a sharp point, the lead breaks off. If you have a small belt sander, chuck the pencil in a portable drill and put the drill in reverse. Turn on the sander and in moments you have a perfect point on the pencil.

plywood, carrying

I don't know just how much a 4×8 sheet of ¾" plywood weighs, but it's difficult for an old guy like me to carry, so I came up with the carrying jig shown. Take a piece of ½" thick plywood that is 12" wide. Put one end of it on the floor and lean it against your leg. Put your arm down and close your hand. Get someone to make a pencil mark on the plywood where your knuckles are. With your square, draw a line 3" below that mark. This will be the top of the hand grip, so the full length of the board will be a couple of inches above that. Drill a starter hole and use a jigsaw to cut out the hand grip. On the bottom of one side, glue and screw two pieces of ¾" plywood that are 2" wide × 12" long. On the bottom of the other side, glue and screw one piece that is also 2" × 12". On top of that piece, place another. Sand off the rough edges and you've got yourself a carrying jig. On one side of the jig, you can carry a ¾" sheet of the plywood. On the other side, you can carry two ½" thick sheets. Just make sure that the sheets are centered on the jig to make it balanced.

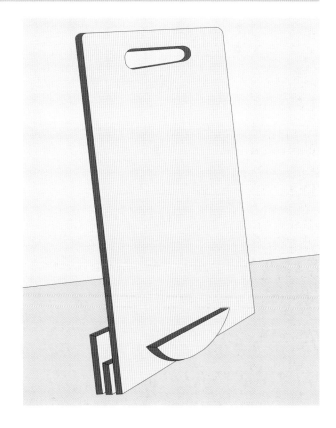

plywood, carrying

Squeeze-type bar clamps can be used as handles for carrying plywood sheets or any other type of flat material.

safety glasses, importance

There is no point to keeping your safety glasses in your tool drawer as the old adage "out of sight, out of mind" will probably apply. I like to keep mine attached to one of the tools that I frequently use, in this case, my compound miter saw. The location almost forces me to put them on. Keep a few extra pairs of safety goggles around the shop. They will come in handy when visitors are working with you. Don't allow anyone near your tools without goggles or a safety visor on. Don't go near a tool without wearing some form of eye protection.

plywood, lifting

Lifting a 4×8 sheet of ¾" plywood onto the table saw top can be a formidable chore at best. Here's a bit of help. Add a couple of small scrap grooved wood blocks to the bottom of your sawhorse legs. Set the end or edge of the plywood sheet on it and then simply tip the horse and the sheet towards your saw.

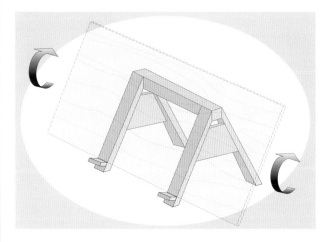

safety glasses, scratching

Stop scratching the lenses of your safety glasses/goggles. The next time one of your socks mysteriously disappears into your dryer, fret not. Use that odd sock to wrap your glasses/goggles in. Now you can safely toss them into your tool box or drawer.

safety glasses, types

There are different types of safety glasses, face shields and goggles available, but before buying any you should make sure that they are safety-certified. The best types are those that protect the temples as well as the eyes. If you wear glasses, there are types that will fit over them. There are also safety glasses that have bi-focal lenses and are available in various strengths. You can extend the life of safety glasses, goggles and face shields by purchasing an inexpensive sheet of thin Lexan polycarbonate. The Lexan polycarbonate can be cut with scissors to the shape of your glasses and taped over the edges of them.

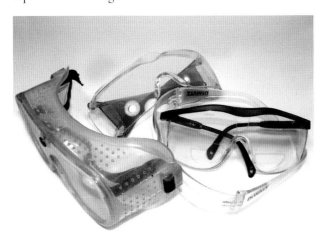

sawdust, for spills

Don't be too quick to empty that sawdust collector. Sawdust is very absorbent and can be used to quickly soak up spilled paints or other finishes in the shop.

sawdust, eye treatment

With sawdust ever present in the workshop, invariably at some point in time you will end up with a speck in your eye, and that is annoying. Don't rub it; instead use a drop or two from a bottle of artificial tears. It will wash that dust speck away. Keep a bottle of it in your first-aid kit.

sawdust, protect calculator

Construction calculators are a real asset in any wood-shop. However, calculators and sawdust do not mix very well. Keep your calculator in a Zip-Lock® freezer bag to protect it. If it is the folding type, keep it open as you will still be able to key into it through the plastic.

sawdust, reducing dust

Keep a plastic pail full of dampened (with water) sawdust in your garage. Sprinkle it on the concrete floor when sweeping up. The damp sawdust will keep the dust down and absorb the fine dirt and dust.

sawdust, separate walnut

Walnut sawdust should be kept separate as the gardener will really appreciate it. Walnut is a natural weed killer. Sweep some into the expansion cracks in your sidewalk or driveway. Also, walnut sawdust is toxic to horses, so don't use it for stall bedding.

sawhorses, cushion

Sometimes you have to put finished pieces on sawhorses and there is always the danger that they can get scratched. Keep a couple of 2×4s wrapped in carpet remnants on hand. Stapling will keep the carpet secure and clamps will hold the pads to the sawhorses.

sawhorses, folding

Most sawhorses take up a lot of room in a small workshop. An easy way of keeping them out of the way is to build them so that they fold up. Make two parts for each sawhorse and run a piano hinge down the center to connect them. A chain and some hooks attached to the legs will keep them from opening too far.

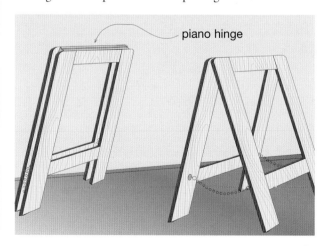

piano hinge

sawhorses, folding

The sawhorse pictured is a different type of folding sawhorse. I came up with this idea when I had a bunch of cabinet carcasses to build. My shop was not big, so the sawhorse had to fold up when not in use. You can use 1×4s or 2×4s to make it; the joints are half-lap and the main beam is 6' long. The swing-arms are 30" long; they can be attached with either butt hinges or piano hinges. This is a surprisingly steady rig that worked well for me.

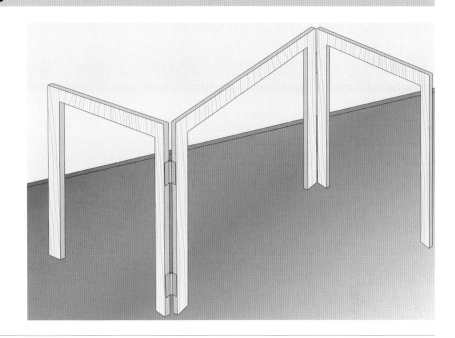

seat, shop made

Standing on a hard wooden or cement floor for long periods of time is eventually going to take its toll on your back. Precisely for that reason, I designed and built the high stool shown here. The stool is made of scrap pieces of spruce and other softwoods. The footrest is from an old broom handle. The stool works well, although I find that the seat (made from glued-up plywood) is a little hard. Someday, I'll put some foam on it and maybe cover it with a vinyl or cloth material. I made the stool high enough so that I can sit comfortably at the workbench or the scroll saw to do carving, scrolling and other relaxing things. The foot rest brings my knees up and makes for a more comfortable sitting position. The stool is an important tool around the shop.

stabilizer

footrest

footrest

shop vacuum, filter upgrade

Make your shop vacuum even more efficient. Get hold of a paper bag for an upright domestic vacuum. These are considerably less expensive than new pleated ones for the shop vacuum. Clean the pleated filter as best you can and then cut the paper filter so that it will fit over it. Use the existing retaining ring to keep it all together.

signing your work

Identify your work! Use a Dremel Motor Tool with the appropriate bit or a Dremel Engraver to sign and date your newly created workpiece in an inconspicuous place. You may also want to add other pertinent details such as the wood species and finish materials.

signing your work

After your project is completed, it is important to keep a permanent record of the materials used to build it. Use a large adhesive label to type or write pertinent information on it and then stick it in an inconspicuous place on the workpiece. Add information like the build date, type of wood used, special hardware and the finishing process and products. Apply several coats of clear finish over the label for permanency.

signing your work

Some woodworkers go to some expense to buy branding irons or some other paraphernalia to proudly sign and date their work. Here's an easier way to date the work. A ¾" Forstner bit will do to drill a shallow hole in the base of the piece. Take a currently dated penny (or other coin) and insert it into the hole. Now you know when the project was built. An indelible marker can be used to sign it.

signing your work

To identify projects that are built by you, go to your computer and design a logo that is unique to you. Add other pertinent details about the work piece and print it on a business-size card. Use a plastic product called Mod Podge (www. plaidonline.com) that will both glue and cover the card to preserve it.

small items, storing

To store items like tie wraps, pencils, tongue depressors, etc., use PVC pipe lengths. Cut one end at 90 degrees and the other at 15 degrees. Use the appropriate-sized hole saw to drill holes at a 15° angle into a length of 1×4. Insert the pipe and mount the piece on a wall. If you don't have the exact size hole saw, use one a little larger; put a screw in the bottom gap and use Gorilla glue to hold the pipe in position.

small items, spray painting

The problem with spray-painting small parts like drawer handles with a compressor-powered spray gun or an aerosol spray can is that the air pressure behind the spray tends to blow the parts all over the place. The other problem is that you usually have to do one side at a time. Next time you have some of these small parts to paint, tap a small nail into the bottom of them or use their packaged screws to secure them and then set them on a piece of nylon fly screen. A pushpin might work if the parts are made of wood. The fly screen should be stapled to some sort of frame for stability. The advantage of the screen is that you don't get the usual accumulation of paint that sticks under the sprayed part.

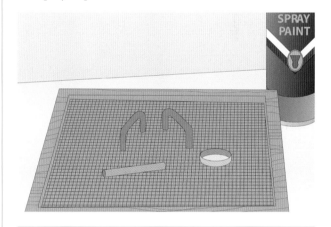

small items, storing

Coffee cans are handy containers for keeping nails, screws and odd small parts. The problem with them is that you can't readily see into them to identify the contents. Build a rack out of scrap wood and do it so that the cans are on a 45° angle.

splinter removing

Working with wood is always pleasurable unless of course you get a splinter of oak or other species stuck in your thumb. Here's an easy way to get rid of it. Put a drop of either white or yellow wood glue on the splinter and then cover it with a Band-Aid® and leave it on overnight. When you remove the bandage in the morning the splinter should come with it.

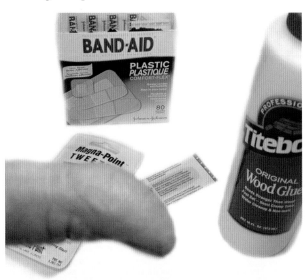

squeegee, shop made

In the event of a wet basement or garage floor, you can make an emergency squeegee by putting a length of foam pipe insulation on the tines of a garden rake.

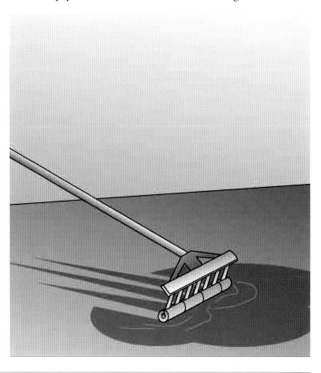

wall cabinet, brackets/french cleat

Here's a dandy idea for hanging those tool cabinets on the wall of your workshop. It's not only easy, it's fast. Rip a 45 degree cut in a couple of 1×2s, full length. Cut a piece to size, that is, the width of your cabinet. Glue and screw it to the back of the cabinet at the top. Cut another piece the same length and screw it to the wall where you want the top of the cabinet to be. Hang the cabinet and you're done. Once you see how easy it is to make these brackets, you'll find more cabinets to hang this way. They are called French cleats.

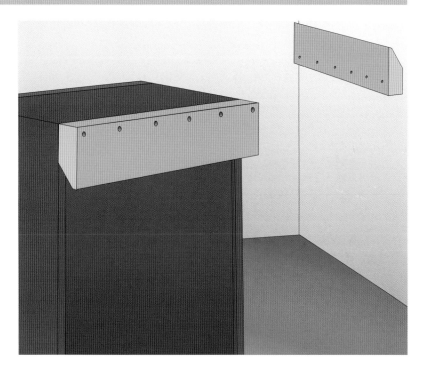

workbench, bench dogs

Workbench vise dogs can sometimes mar a workpiece. To help prevent this from happening, cover the ends of the dogs with neoprene tubing (available at your plastics dealer) or other resilient material.

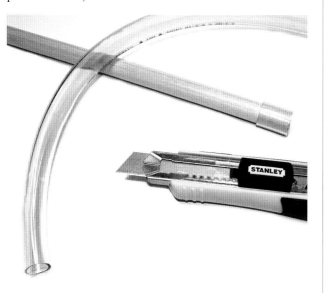

workbench, bench dogs

There is an old adage that you can't fit a square peg into a round hole. This may be true but you can fit a round peg into a square hole. If necessary, add a "shim" to the peg so it will fit tightly into the hole.

workbench, bench hooks

Here's a tool that I haven't used since my days in grade school, but it's still useful to have around the shop when you can't find elusive bench dogs. Using a good grade (clear) of ¾" plywood, cut a piece 8" × 12" and sand its surfaces and edges smooth. Cut two pieces of ¾" scrap plywood 8" long × 1½" wide. Glue and screw one piece flush along the short edge of the plywood, turn it over and do the same thing on the other side and the opposite end. Now you have a bench hook. It can be used on your workbench with the bottom 1" × ¼" piece hooked against the edge of the bench. Thus the name bench hook. Now, you can use it for miter-or square-cutting with your hacksaw, or as a brace for chisel work or planing. Like most of my jigs, I drill a hole in it near the top so I can hang it up on a pegboard.

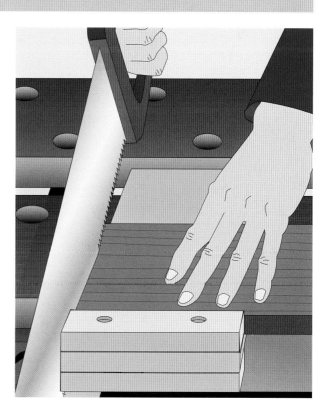

workbench, bench hook

Here's another type of bench hook: Follow the directions for the previous bench hook, but on one side, or edge, make a 45 degree cut near one corner. Right-handers should make the cut on the right side of the boards, and left-handers on the left side. This will give you a fairly accurate mitered cut.

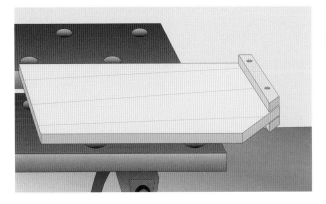

workbench, light

To add more light to your workbench, do the following: Install a drapery I-beam above and running the length of your workbench. Run a lamp wire through the roller loops, attach a lamp socket and shade on one end and a plug on the other. Gently squeeze the loops so that they grab the wire. Be careful: Don't break the outer cover of the wire.

workbench, expanding space

An old hollow-core interior door can be used to greatly extend the surface of your workbench. Use a piano hinge to fasten it to the edge of your bench so that it will swing down and out of the way. Hinge a couple of 2×4s under the door for support legs when it is in use. Flip the supports up and drop the door to get it out of the way.

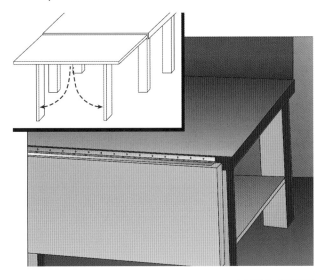

workmate, extender

The Workmate has been used by do-it-yourselfers and woodworkers for many years and has become a great substitute for a full-blown workbench. Although it is a versatile tool that should find a place in any workshop, it does have its limits. The illustrated Workmate extenders are easily shop built and will give it a larger holding capacity. Build them to a length that suits you. The extenders use ¾" plywood and dowels or pieces of an old broomstick.

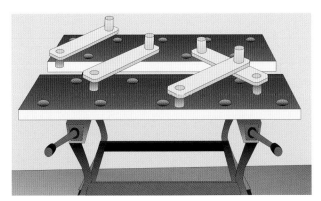

workmate, extenders

In this second version, also use a piece of ¾"
plywood; it should be approximately 30" ×
30". This will make a good-sized work surface. On the underside of the plywood, glue
and screw a strip of ¾" plywood that is 4"
wide × 30" long. Run it down the middle.
Cut one more piece of ¾" plywood that is 5"
wide × 30" long. Before gluing and screwing it onto the narrower piece, check the
thickness of the Workmate's jaws. Mine are
made of ⅞" plywood, so I shimmed my work
surface with a piece of ⅛" plywood. This T-
shaped piece will now hold the work surface
securely in the jaws of the Workmate. Sand
and finish the top surface, and you have a
portable workbench.

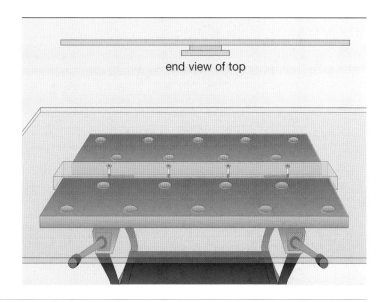

end view of top

workmate, nail support bin

Many manufacturers sell
clip-on containers that fit
onto brackets. These brackets hook onto pegboards.
This is very convenient
when you are working
within the confines of your
workshop. However, during
the warm months you may
have several woodworking
projects to do outdoors.
Running back and forth to
your workshop to get six
or more screws or nails is
not my idea of a good time.
The solution is to bring
them with you. The storage
containers have a built-in

clip on their backside, for hanging. Here's a way for
hanging them on the cross-brace of your Workmate:
Purchase aluminum angles from hardware stores or
your local aluminum distributor (you might also try
an aluminum window and door retailer). The 1 × 1
× 40" angles are sold by either weight or foot and
range in length from 8' to 20' or more. Rest assured,
the unused portion will not be wasted. Cut a length

equal to the crossbar on your Workmate. Turn your
Workmate upside down. Set the aluminum angle on
the underside of the crossbar. Drill 3 or 4 holes that
are the size of your pop rivets (blind rivets) and install
the angle. When you turn the unit upright, you now
have a bracket on which to install your nail or parts
bins. This will save a lot of time when using your
Workmate away from your shop.

workmate, tool rack

The tool rack shown is an easy-to-make accessory for your Workmate. The rack is made of ¾" plywood. Appropriate-sized holes are drilled to facilitate your selection of tools. The beauty of it is that it can easily be lifted off when not in use.

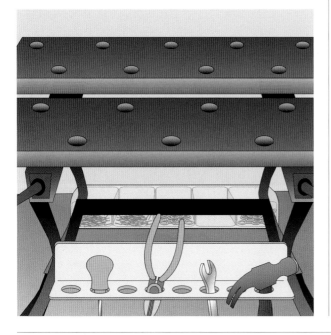

workshop, cleaning

Using an old leaf rake with a shortened handle will gather pieces of wood on your shop floor so they don't clog your shop vacuum.

workshop, cleaning

A good shop-type vacuum is the best way to clean up your shop. Unlike a push broom, it creates no dust and, of course, can get into those little nooks and crannies that a broom can't. I am usually in my shop six days a week, so I generally dedicate one morning per week to cleaning up. One of what I consider the most important cleanup jobs is the cleaning of my power tools. It is amazing how much damage sawdust can do to your tools. You will probably extend the life of these tools threefold by giving them a regular vacuuming. Pay particular attention to the motor housings. Put the vacuum nozzle up tight to the openings to clean out the dust and debris.

TECHNIQUES

drilling, cleaning holes

Drilling a series of holes for adjustable shelves can sometimes leave shavings in the holes that are difficult to get out. Talk to your dentist, he/she would be very happy to give you their old stainless steel dental picks. These are great for probing into those holes.

drilling, holes saws

If you are having trouble removing those wood plugs from a hole saw, use a couple of 2½" deck screws. Drive the screws into the plug and as they hit bottom on the hole saw they will force the plug out.

drilling, parking drill

Keep your corded or cordless drill "parked" for readily convenient use. To do this, screw a scrap of 2×4 to the back of your workbench. Drive a nail or nails into the piece and cut the head(s) off. The drills can now be chucked onto the headless nails to keep them handy. If they are corded, simply leave a little more space to allow the wires to run around the back and hang over the bench edge.

drilling, perpendicular holes

The electric drill was probably the first portable power tool invented. I am not sure when this tool was first put on the market, but it still has major drawbacks that have not been improved on. It is difficult to drill a truly perpendicular hole in a workpiece with a portable drill. Many manufacturers have come up with a myriad of ideas that would "guarantee" perpendicular holes every time, but most of these ideas have meant either dismantling the drill chuck or attaching (with straps, screws, nuts and bolts) some elaborate gizmo or some sort of flimsy drill-press type of attachment. Here's a technique that won't take long, costs very little, and does not require any elaborate installation. It's a V-block. The block is made from a piece of scrap hardwood and can be clamped to your workpiece. All you have to do is make sure that the drill bit is kept snug in the wedge.

drilling, repeat holes with a portable drill

Making a series of equally-spaced holes is easy using the jig shown here. Let's assume that the required holes are ¼" in diameter and spaced 3" apart. Take a piece of scrap ¾" thick plywood and cut it 3" square. Make a mark ½" in from either end and ½" across. This will give you 2" centers. Drill a ¼" hole at these marks. A Forstner bit works best because it produces very clean cuts. Insert a ¼" dowel into one of the holes. The length of the dowel should be 1" with about ¼" protruding. You may have to glue it in place. Determine where your first hole is going to be and drill it. Place the dowel of the jig in the hole and place a straightedge against the jig and clamp it parallel to the edge of your workpiece. Drill the second hole through the hole in the jig. Now move the jig and place the dowel in the second hole and drill the next hole and so on.

drilling, starter hole

Always make a starter hole when drilling with a conventional twist drill bit to prevent possible drill bit wandering. In addition, this will insure a clean entry. Use an awl to make the starter hole.

gluing fragile parts

Sometimes turnings or carvings accidentally break and they break in areas that are difficult to clamp or at least to hold in position until the glue sets. This idea may help. Glue up the edges of the pieces using wood glue and wipe off any squeeze out. Use a hot melt glue gun to place dabs of hot glue in strategic places until the wood glue sets. Then the hot melt glue can be easily scraped off.

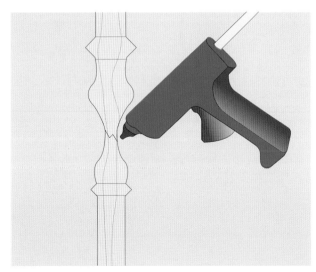

nailing, close to edges

You have to drive a nail through a board and you are only a ½" or so away from the edge. You know that the board is going to split. As a matter of fact, you can probably sense it before you even put the hammer to it. I'm not guaranteeing this technique will work all the time, but it's worth the risk: Before driving the nail(s), flatten the point with a hammer and then place the nail with the flattened end across the wood grain. The same applies when nailing into the end grain of a piece of wood such as a 2×4.

nailing, close quarters

Here is an effective technique involving using either a C-clamp or slip-joint pliers to "squeeze" a nail in place when using a hammer could split the wood.

nailing, correct way

To obtain a tight nail joint, there is a correct way of driving nails. Let's assume that you want to join a 1×4 to the end of another 1×4, to make a right angle. First, select a nail that is a length equal to two times the thickness of the board, in this case, a 1½" finishing nail. A 4"-wide board should take three or four nails, equally spaced. Drive the nail until it just protrudes from the underside, making sure that the nail is perpendicular to the work. Now, line up the two boards and finish driving in the nail. The remaining two or three nails should be driven in at opposing angles of about 15 degrees. The result will be a secure joint. Of course, a little glue before nailing is added security.

nailing, finished wood

Sometimes finishing nails are required for the final assembly of your finished project. Hammering in finishing nails can be hazardous in that one slip of the hammer can result in a dimple that is very difficult to repair. This technique will prevent a lot of frustration: Place a shim or a piece of wood shingle on the part to be nailed and then simply drive the nail through the shim and into your workpiece. When the nail is driven into the workpiece, just break off the shim and use a nail set to complete the job.

nailing, guard

There is another method of protecting your workpiece. Don't throw those scrap pieces of pegboard into the kindling bin just yet, especially if you are doing some finish-nailing. Pegboard strips are ideal makeshift nailing protectors. Simply start your nail, hang the pegboard strip on it and drive it home. The remaining ¼" or so should be driven in with a nail set. Don't try this with common nails unless you can fit the nail head through the pegboard hole.

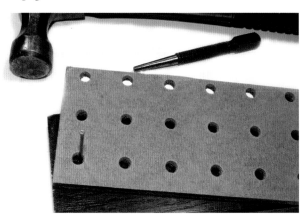

nailing, guard

Shown here is a helpful little nailing guard that you can make in a couple of minutes. It will safely prevent inadvertent dings in your workpiece and help you to keep your nails straight. Cut a piece of ¼"-thick Plexiglas or Lexan 2" wide × about 8" long. Sand the edges and slightly round off the corners. Make a slot about halfway up the middle of the guard with your band saw. That's all there is to it. Place your nail in the slot, line it up on your workpiece and hammer it in. Do not hammer it all the way in; keep the head just above the Plexiglas to allow you to remove the Plexiglas. Finish nailing with a nail set.

nailing, nail holder

Small alligator clips, available at places like Radio Shack, can be used to hold small finishing nails when there is a fear of hitting your thumb with the hammer.

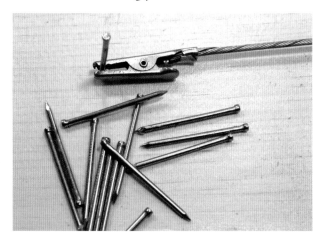

nailing, nail sets

Nail sets can be found in a variety of sizes and are generally used to set finishing nails below the surface. It is important to select the right size for the nail diameter that you are using, otherwise, the nail set may leave a larger hole than desired. If the nail set is too small, it could slip off the nail and cause damage.

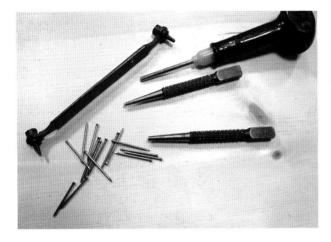

nail, removing

Those spiral and ring-type nails can be a problem to remove because of their grip in the wood. Use a pair of Vise-Grips to grasp the nail and pry it out and use a piece of scrap to protect the piece.

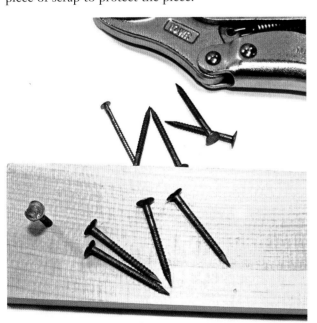

nail, removing

Removing different types of nails safely takes a variety of methods for specific nail types. For example, some common and spiral nails should be pulled by the head with a hammer claw. A scrap of wood placed under the hammerhead will protect the surface. If you have to remove a nail from a piece of moulding, you should remove the entire piece and pull the nails through the underside of the moulding. This prevents tear-out on the surface. Air nailers pose another problem. The heads are so small that a hammer claw won't grip them and if you try to hammer them out from underneath, they are sure to bend. A brad pusher will keep the nails straight and push them through. A pair of Vise-Grips will then pull the nail out.

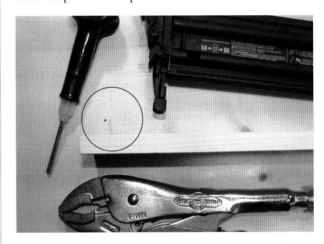

nail, removing

To help in removing nails from recycled wood, use conventional wood shims or a wood scrap to increase your hammer's leverage.

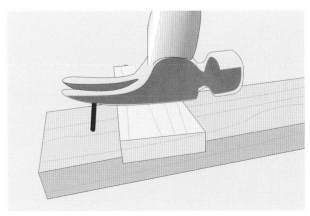

nail, sizing

Before you drive that nail into your project, think about the size of the nail you are using. To achieve the strongest joint, the nails should penetrate about two-thirds to three-quarters into the lower piece.

nail, toenailing

Toe nailing a 2×4 stud into the sole plate usually makes the stud slip out of position a little. The reason for this is that it takes a few hits with the hammer for the nail to bite. Here's a trick of the trade I learned while visiting a job site: If you turn the nail upside down and hit it on the edge of its head, the result will be a "pocket." Now, turn the nail the right way and drive it home.

routing small parts

Routing small parts is made safer and easier if they are clamped flush to the router table in a hand screw. The router bit may chew up a bit of the wood of the clamp but that is better than chewing up your fingers.

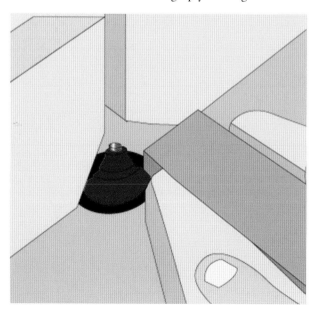

sanding, concave surfaces

Hand-sanding concave surfaces can be difficult because it is difficult to maintain the flat shape of the edge with your finger wrapped in sandpaper; as one would normally do. Try this shortcut next time: Take a piece of dowel as close as possible in diameter to what you want to sand. Wrap a piece of sandpaper around it, grit side out, and leave a "tail" at each end so that they may be clamped together. Or, wrap sandpaper around an old butt hinge and tighten the paper and hinge with a small bolt and wing nut.

sanding, drywall joints

When sanding drywall joints either by hand or with a sander, a lot of dust is created. To keep the dust down to a minimum, cut the bottom of a plastic windshield-wiper fluid bottle. Remove the cap and use duct tape to attach the cap end to a shop vacuum. Hold the bottle just below the area that you are sanding. Note: Gypsum board (Gyproc) dust can be very damaging to a vacuum, so do not use your home vacuum cleaner for this.

sanding, preventing marks

When sanding a horizontal surface close to vertical edges, like inside a drawer or cabinet, a random-orbital sander can leave deep marks when you sand too close. A thin piece of cardboard taped to the vertical edge will prevent this.

sanding, substitute

Like most woodworkers, I have a great variety of sandpaper products ranging from belts, discs, rolls and sheets. But, there are times when none of the above will really work in a given situation. Sometimes you need to get in close and tight. I always keep a selection of emery boards on hand. They work in a pinch.

sanding, small parts

There are times when you have to use your stationary belt sander to clean a small part. These little parts have a tendency to slip between the fence and the sanding belt. To prevent this, clamp a piece of ¼"-thick plywood, that is as wide as the belt, to the sander's fence. Clamp it so it is snug against the sanding belt. Then carefully sand your small workpiece. The additional fence will prevent your workpiece from sliding under the metal fence.

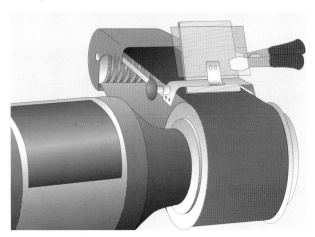

sanding, sureform

Is that interior door that you just installed hanging just a tad too low in spots for your liking? Don't remove it! More than likely a Sureform® blade will take care of the problem with the door still in position.

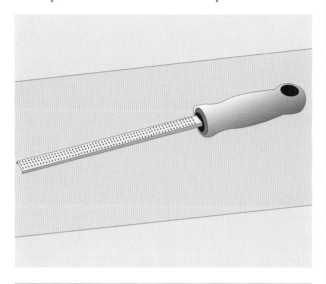

screws, driving in tight spots

Those short five-sided bits that come with cordless screwdrivers will fit nicely into a ¼" socket. A socket wrench is just the thing if you are working in tight corners or where the height is restricted.

screws, driving in hardwood

Driving screws into hardwood can be difficult at the best of times, even with a pilot hole drilled. This technique will make things a little easier for you: Keep a wax candle, some beeswax or a block of paraffin wax near your screw cabinet. After you have drilled your pilot hole, apply any of the above to the screw threads and proceed to drive the screw. You will find a big difference in the effort required.

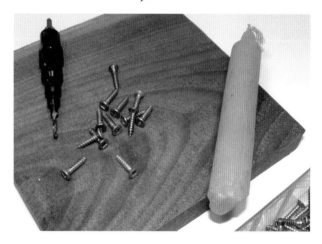

screws, lubricating

Wood screws will go into hardwoods much easier if they are lubricated. An easy way of doing this is to buy a toilet bowl wax seal. When you are ready to assemble that project, put the screws into the wax to keep them handy for use and lubrication at the same time. Keep the wax seal in a closed container for future use.

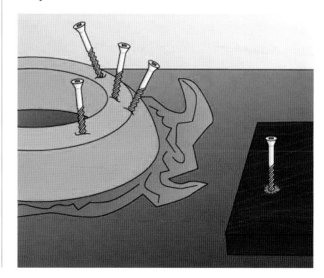

screws, measuring

When is a 2" screw not a 2" screw? When it's a pan-head screw! Care should be taken when using a tape measure to verify the length of screws because the measurements vary with the type of screw being measured. As an example, a roundhead screw is measured from under the head, while a flathead screw is measured from the top of the head.

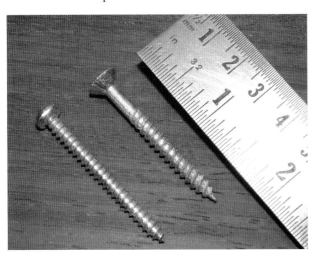

screw plugs, trimming

Trimming screw plugs can be made clean and simple with your dozuki saw. Use an old perforated sanding disc with the fabric side up to prevent marring your workpiece. One of the holes in the disc should fit nicely on the dowel. Sanding will clean it all up.

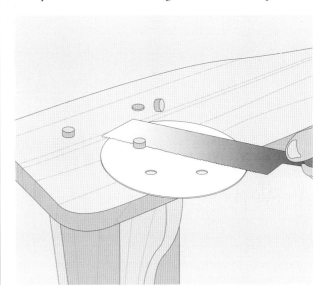

screws, removing broken

A bent or broken screw is always a woodworker's nightmare, especially in a nearly finished project. A screw with a stripped head is just as annoying. Don't get upset about it, as this workshop technique may solve the problem. The drill/driver that you used to install the screw in the first place is probably the best tool for removing the damaged screw. Remove the screwdriver bit from your drill and then set the drill chuck over the screw. Tighten the chuck snugly and then put the drill in reverse. This should do the trick.

stripped head   broken screw

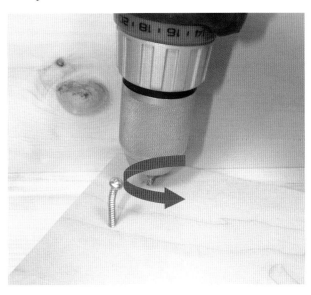

screws, repairing broken

It can be very annoying when a screw breaks off as a project is being assembled. The removal of it can cause a lot of damage to the project. Here's a way of removing the screw and causing minimal damage. Drill small diagonal holes around the perimeter of the screw so that you can get a pair of needle-nose pliers in there to grip and remove the broken screw. Once the screw is out, enlarge the screw hole to the diameter of a small dowel. Cut the dowel to a length that fits flush with the surface and then glue it into position. When the glue dries, use a countersink bit to recess the new screw and then counterbore for a larger screw. Once the new, larger screw is set, use a plug cutter on a piece of similar scrap wood and cover up the screw with the plug.

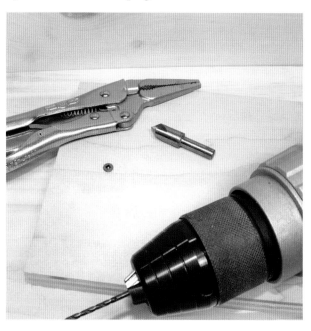

spirals, making

Some neat things such as salad bowls, decorative cones, etc., can be made from spirals. To draw a spiral, wrap a piece of string around a nail and tie the loose end to a pencil. Using the pencil, start drawing a circle from the nail that is fixed to the middle of your workpiece. As you rotate the pencil around the nail, the string will start wrapping around the nail, making the string shorter as you go. These are the cutting lines. Tilt your band saw table to the desired angle that you want the bowl or cone to be, and proceed to cut from the outside line. Once the cut is complete, turn off the saw and slowly start to retract the blade by backing up through the cut. Place a dowel or a tin can under the center of the workpiece and carefully pull the coil down, clamping it to a secure surface. A little glue before clamping will hold it together.

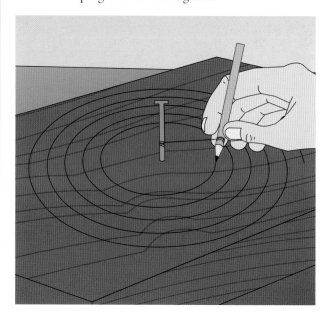

screws, tightening

It is easy to repair a project that has loose screws. A roll of edge veneer — the type with the hot-melt glue on the back — will do the trick nicely. Cut a few wedge-shaped pieces off the roll and insert them into the screw hole. Driving the screw back in will soften or even melt the glue and hold the screw firmly.

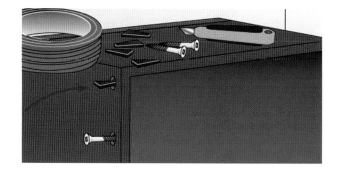

squaring project corners

With a tape measure or a string, measure diagonally across two opposite corners. Mark the string and measure the other two corners. The measurements should be identical.

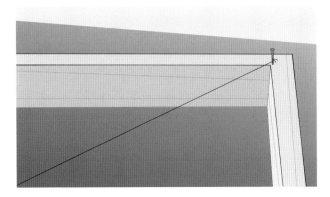

tear-out, preventing

Crosscutting plywood with less than an 80-tooth, carbide-tipped saw blade will invariably cause tear out (rough edges), but not all of us have or can afford such a blade. Here is a technique that will save you both time and money the next time you are crosscutting a piece of plywood. Run a strip of masking tape across the width of the workpiece where your cutline will be. Draw your line on the masking tape and make the cut, also cutting the masking tape. The result will be a nice, clean cut. The downside to this technique is that you will probably have to clean your saw blade more often, but if you are making a lot of these crosscuts, it's worth it. You won't have to spend time filling the chipped areas with wood filler either.

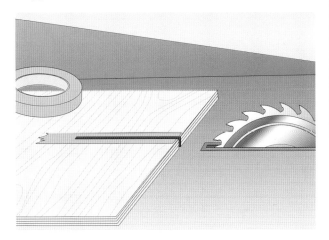

squaring project corners

This method is called the 3-4-5 method and it is basic. Start at one corner of the piece. At the right of the corner, make a mark exactly at 3". At the left of the corner, make a mark exactly at 4". Now, measure diagonally across to the two lines. This measurement should read 5" exactly. Double-check by repeating this at the opposite corner.

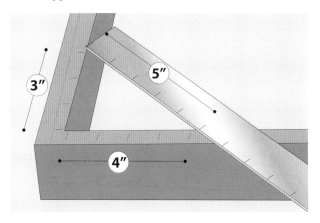

wheels, shop made

Here is a quick way to make a dozen or so toy wheels. Select a piece of wood stock that is about ¼" thicker than the wheels you want to produce. It should be long and wide enough to accommodate the required quantity. Set up your drill press with the appropriate hole saw and set your depth adjustment to stop the drill press ⅛" or ¼" from drilling through the workpiece. Cut the wheels, then use your band saw to resaw the wheels free of the piece of wood. A little sanding and you're ready to roll.

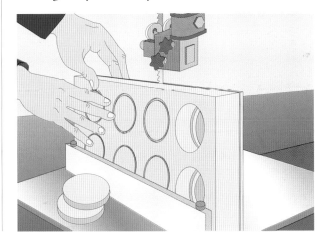

TOOLS

allen keys, improving

Many of the tools that you buy require assembly and the manufacturers usually include some of the tools to do it. The tools will no doubt include an Allen key or two. These Allen keys are usually L-shaped and the "L" can get in the way. Cut the "L" out of it (pun intended). The straight shaft will fit nicely into a portable drill and will give you that much more torque for assembly.

awl, sharpening

Check the point of the awl from time to time, especially after using it on metals, to make sure that it is sharp. The awl can be easily sharpened on a belt or disc sander using fine-grit sandpaper. Be careful, though: Don't let it get too hot when sharpening because it will lose its temper and won't be as effective when scribing metals.

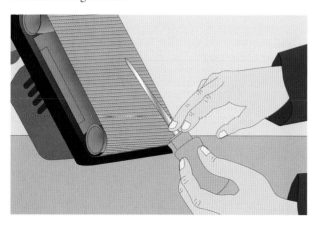

awl, marking

The awl, also known as a scratch awl, is a tool that no home workshop should be without. The awl has many uses; it can be used in lieu of a pencil for drawing or scribing lines on wood, plastics and metals. On darker woods such as mahogany or rosewood, a scribe stands out better than a pencil line.

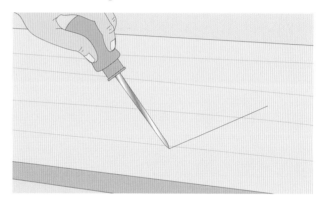

band saw, auxilliary table

An auxiliary table for a band saw, especially a removable one like the one shown here, is a great advantage to the woodworker. It is particularly useful for cutting large circles for tabletops, etc. One way to make an auxiliary table is to laminate two pieces of ¾"-thick plywood to make a 1½"-thick slab and screw a piece of aluminum angle to both sides. Drill holes into the edge of the saw table castings and make slots in the aluminum angle to correspond. Put hinged legs on the table so it can fold up when not in use. It only takes a couple of minutes to set it up with ¼" bolts and wing nuts.

band saw, backtracking

Let's say, for example, that you are going to cut the outside of the letter "U" with a band saw. You know that you are going to have trouble making the turn because of the width of the blade that you have in the saw. There are three ways of making the cut: Making three straight cuts and then going back and nibbling at the rounded comers; cutting straight down the sides and backtracking out so you can make a straight cut across the bottom, and then nibbling at the rounded comers; and the easiest way, which consists of making your first cut straight down the side, backtracking about an inch, and slowly starting to nibble away at the rounded corner. Repeat at the next turn and you have a perfect U. Backtracking out of a cut can be difficult. What usually happens is the kerf closes up, binding the blade, and you end up pulling the moving blade out of the guide blocks. You will also move the blade off the crest of the tire and loosen the tension of the blade, probably causing it to come off the wheels altogether and, at worst, breaking the blade. So, it is best to backtrack only when necessary.

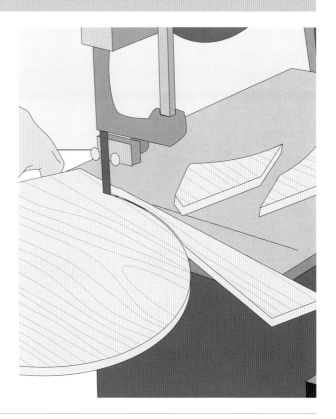

band saw, blade types

Band-saw blades come in a variety of lengths, widths and tooth counts. They range in width from ³⁄₃₂" to 3". The latter can be found at some sawmills. The minimum and maximum blade widths will depend on the specifications for your band saw. The type of blade to use will depend on the type of work that has to be done. A narrower blade will cut smaller diameters. A ½"- to 1"-wide blade will be best for resawing. Blade lengths also vary, depending on the make and type of saw. If you are buying new blades for a saw that uses a 97" long blade, a 96" or 98" blade will probably work. The blade tension can be adjusted to make up the difference. The tooth count is another factor. The tooth count is the number of teeth per inch on the blade. The more teeth, the finer and slower the cut. Less teeth will give a faster but rougher cut. A skip-tooth blade is used for ripping. It is best suited for cutting soft metals such as aluminum.

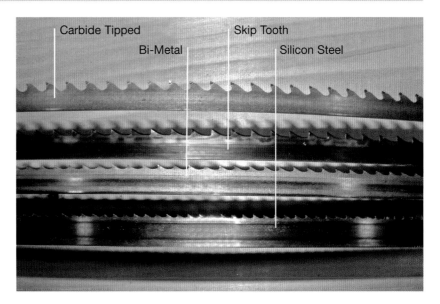

Carbide Tipped   Skip Tooth
    Bi-Metal   Silicon Steel

band saw, cutting accuracy

Like many power tools that you buy, you can't just open the box the band saw comes in and start using the saw. It's a tool that will give precision cuts if tuned and adjusted correctly. Follow the manufacturer's instructions precisely when setting it up. By doing this, you will ensure accurate cuts. The simple procedure of changing a blade could have an effect on the saw's accuracy. So, there are six very important steps that you should perform after every blade change. The following must be done with the tool unplugged:

1 With a wood chisel braced on the upper frame, check for roundness of the upper wheel. Doing this will also remove any sawdust buildup on the wheel's tire. Any unevenness may be marked and sanded down with fine sandpaper. Repeat the process for the bottom (drive) wheel. A light sanding with 180- to 220-grit sandpaper should remove any sawdust or other adherents.

2 Check the new blade for any defects, especially at the welded joint. If there are any high spots or roughness at the weld, grind them down. This will save wear and tear on the rubber tires and the guide blocks.

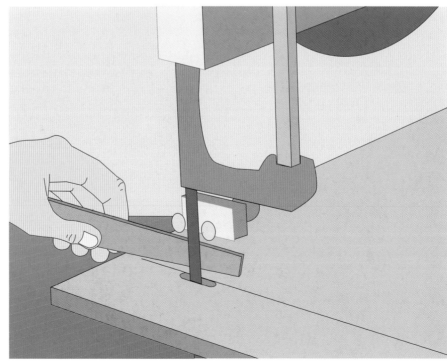

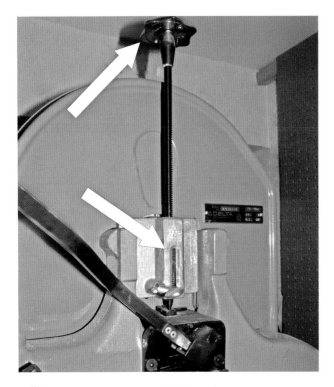

3 Install the blade and adjust the tension just enough to hold the blade in place. Rotate the upper wheel to be certain that the blade is riding dead center on the tires. Adjust the upper-wheel pivot so the blade tracks properly. Tighten the tension screw for the blade to the appropriate mark.

4 Adjust the guide blocks so that they sit just behind the gullets of the blade and don't make contact with the teeth.

5 Adjust the bearing wheels so they just touch the back of the saw blade.

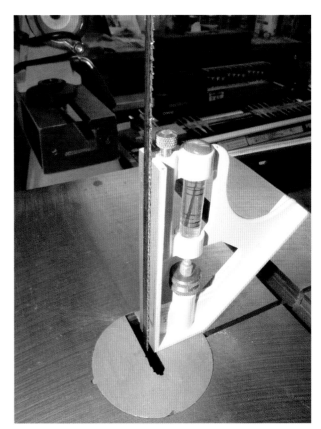

6 Raise the blade guide to its uppermost position. Using a try square, verify the squareness of the blade to the saw table. Adjust the table accordingly and reset the table stop if required.

band saw, cutting circles

When cutting large circles on a band saw, look at your squared piece of stock carefully. If, for example, you are using softwood and there are lots of knots in it, choose another piece. If the wood is relatively unblemished, make sure that you start your cut at about a 45-degree angle and into a cross-grain area. The reason for this is that the blade may pull slightly if the initial cut is with the grain. More important, don't skimp on the material. If you want to cut a 12"-diameter circle, your stock should be at least 13" square. This will allow for a continuous cut, rather than a tight cut that will leave you with flat spots that require sanding later. When cutting large circles, such as tabletops, use an auxiliary table. Find the center of your stock and drill a small hole there. Start your cut and then drive a nail through the hole and into your auxiliary table. Make sure that the nail is in perfect alignment with the teeth of the saw blade and proceed to cut carefully.

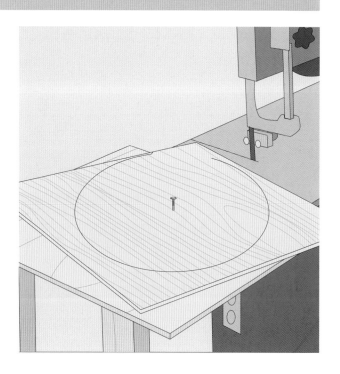

band saw, cutting dowels

To split a short length of dowel with your band saw, cut a V-block as shown here, set your dowel into it, and carefully push the V-block and dowel into the blade. After you have cut about inch, push a small finishing nail through the kerf to keep the dowel vertical. Now, push only the dowel into the blade.

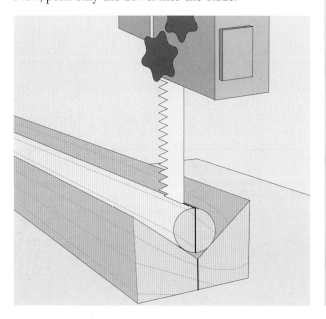

band saw, cutting dowels

Another method for cutting or splitting dowels is to square off a piece of scrap and drill a hole in it that is just slightly larger than the dowel. Hold the scrap tightly against the fence and slowly push the dowel through the hole until you have cut about an inch into the dowel. Now, withdraw the dowel, turn it around, and reinsert it into the scrap. Tap a small nail (the size of the kerf) through the stock into the hole. This will prevent the dowel from twisting. Continue the cut up to the nail, being careful not to strike the nail with the blade. Note: Make sure that the dowel you are splitting is a couple of inches longer than required.

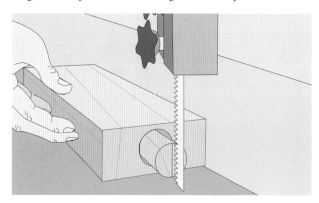

band saw, cutting limits

Band saws are great tools for cutting circles, but the radius of the circle to be cut is limited to the width of the blade that you are using.

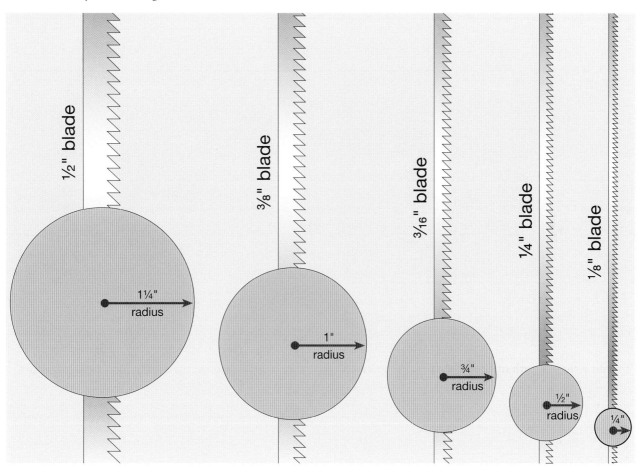

band saw, cutting spirals

Spiraled or fluted dowels are required when making doweled glue joints because they hold the glue better and thus make a stronger joint. Invariably, however, you won't have the type or size of dowel required. If you have a fluting chisel, you can easily make the type of dowel required. If not, try this technique that I learned a few years ago: Tilt the table of your band saw 15 to 20 degrees, use your miter gauge to hold the dowel at a right angle to the saw blade, and turn on the saw. The amount of pressure that you apply toward the blade will determine the depth of the cut. The saw-blade motion will automatically make the spiraling. A little practice and you'll have it down pat.

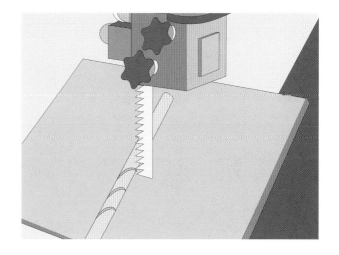

band saw, guide blocks

The standard guide blocks that are usually supplied with a band saw are generally made of metal and they do show signs of wear in time. Do not throw them out. First do the obvious: Turn them around and use the other ends. When the other ends show signs of wear, use a bench-top disc or belt sander to redress them.

band saw, guide blocks

If you happen to live in a coastal area where there are some shipbuilders, boat builders or shipwrights, make use of these resources to make your own Cool Blocks. A lot of these trades use what they call "iron wood." Its proper name is lignum vitae. A couple of scrap pieces of this wood are all that you need to make your own guide blocks.

band saw, guide blocks

Another approach is to use Cool Blocks. Cool Blocks are made from a graphite-impregnated phenolic resin material. They create a lot less heat than conventional guide blocks, which adds to the life of the saw blade. The big advantage is that these blocks can be closed up tighter to the blade and give greater accuracy to the saw cut. Cool Blocks have one other advantage. When you are using a blade narrower than ¼", the blocks can be adjusted to cover the entire blade width without damaging the teeth.

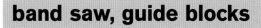

band saw, guide blocks

There are guide blocks available that are cut on a 45-degree angle (or you can make your own). The advantage of having these on hand is that they can be installed to make cuts wider than the saw's throat. If you install these blocks angled so that the teeth of the saw blade are aimed to the right, they will twist the blade to allow a workpiece that is wider than the saw's throat. Caution, however, is required. Make absolutely sure that the blade guard is in its uppermost position.

band saw, installing blades

Installing a band-saw blade was difficult for me until I discovered the method shown here. Place the blade on the top wheel first. Next, using small spring clamps or clothespins, hold the blade securely. Feed it through the guides and over the bottom wheels. Adjust the blade tension, remove the clamps and check for blade centering. The blade is now installed. For optimum performance from a band saw, the blade must be centered on the wheels. The wheels on the band saw have rubber tires on them and these tires are crowned. The blade must ride on the crowns (the center of the tires). The saw has a control (usually on the back of the saw) that will alter the alignment of the top wheel by tilting the wheel in or out. Rotate the top wheel by hand to see how the blade sits. Adjust the control accordingly.

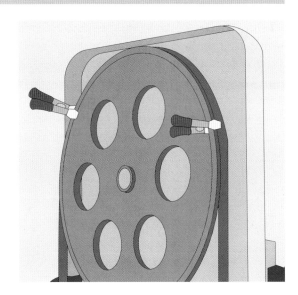

band saw, making long crosscuts

Somebody ought to impeach Mr. Murphy and repeal his laws. They always seem to come up in woodworking. For example: You have a band saw with a 14" throat and, of course, the workpiece that you want to crosscut is 15" or 16" wide. Hold one end of the stock against the support post, line up the back of the cut line with your blade, and pivot the cut through. Then trim off the waste. This shortcut is usually limited to workpieces that are from 3" to 6" in width. If the stock is wider, simply turn it over and repeat the procedure. This will save a lot of scrap that would normally be thrown away.

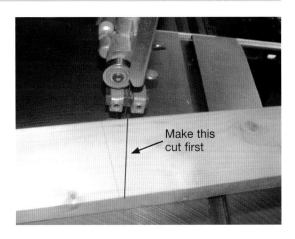

Make this cut first

band saw, making long crosscuts

There is another method of making long crosscuts. This involves a little more work, however. Raise the blade guard as high as it will go. Relieve some of the tension on the blade. Start the cut. When the blade is fully into the workpiece, back up just a little. Turn off the saw. Place the workpiece kerf into the blade and twist the workpiece so that the blade is cutting off square (to the right). The blade should follow the line. The wider the blade, the better. Without question, this method will put extra strain on the blade and the guide blocks, so don't do it too often.

band saw, relief cutting

Making tight turns when cutting with a band saw is easy to do if the correct blade is installed. There are times, however, when we get lazy and try to make cuts with a blade that is too wide. For example, you may want to cut an oval (ellipse) and know the blade that is in the saw will easily cut the sides, but will not be able to turn tight enough to cut the top without binding. This shortcut will save some time, irritation, your saw guide blocks and probably the blade: Before starting to cut the ellipse, make some relief cuts right up to the pattern line at the top and the bottom of the pattern. The cuts should be at a slight angle to the line. The more cuts that you make, the easier it will be on the blade and the saw. Now, when making these tight turns, the scrap will just break away and ease the tension on the blade.

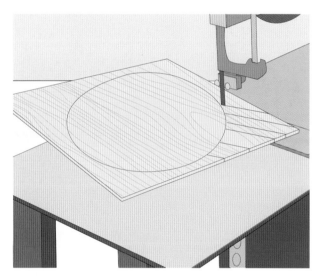

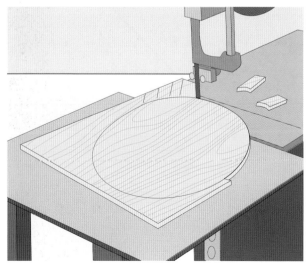

band saw, resawing

Resawing in woodworking terms is considered the ability to cut a 4×4 (nominal measurement) into four 2×2 pieces. This is done on the band saw. It can also be a precision technique in which woodworkers slice a piece 1/32" wide off the face of a 1 × 8" board. Needless to say, to accomplish this both the table and the blade must be accurate and the widest blade possible for your machine is required. After you have checked the level of the table and the plumb of the blade, the next thing is to make sure that your rip fence is square to the table. There may be times when you want to resaw a piece that is 4" high and your rip fence is only 2" high. This shortcut will help: Either use your thickness planer or have your lumberyard mill a piece of elm or maple to precisely 1" in thickness. Failing this, a piece of plywood will do. This stock should be 6" wide and at least twice the length of your saw table. Affix the stock to your existing fence with nuts and recessed bolts. The reason for using stock 1" thick is to ensure its rigidity. If the measurement scale on the rip fence is accurate, subtract 1" from the indicated mark.

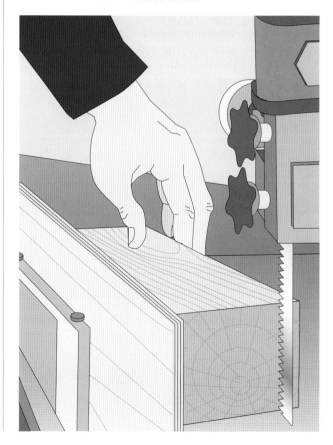

band saw, rip fence

I made the band saw rip fence shown here from ¾" plywood, an aluminum angle bracket and a long carriage bolt with a wing nut. Though I had to cut out an area for the blade guard, the fence works well and took less than an hour to make. Before ripping, make sure the fence is square to the table.

band saw, rounding blades

Rounding the back edges of your band-saw blades will help to make the blades cut smoother, reduce the wear on the guide blocks and extend the life of the blades. This is easy to do. With the machine turned on, carefully apply a sharpening stone to the back edges of the blade in a rounding motion. With narrower blades, slowly feed a piece of scrap wood into the blade while you are rounding them. This will prevent the blade from twisting.

band saw, scoring for a straight line

How often have we taken out the tape measure to make a mark, say 6'1" on a 1×4 piece of stock? Well, we make the mark, find our try square, draw a line and then proceed to make the final cut. This technique will save you from having to root around your toolbox or going over to your pegboard to find the try square. Simply make your measured pencil mark at the top edge of your workpiece and advance the piece into the moving band-saw blade, just enough to score it. Now, turn it up so that the score line is on top and proceed to follow that line with your cut. If your saw is properly set up, you will end up with a perfectly square end.

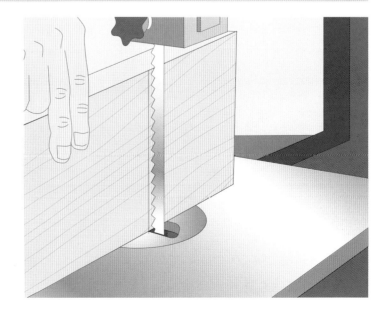

band saw, tensioning blade

A properly tensioned blade will give a more accurate cut and last longer than an improperly tensioned one. Most band saws have a scale either printed or molded right by the blade-tensioning screw. In most cases, this scale gives only a general indication of the tension of the blade. A good industrial-type blade will usually take considerably much more tension than what the scale indicates. So, if you want to ensure straight and accurate cuts without the blade wandering or following the wood grain, tighten up your blade. If, for example, you have installed a ¼" blade, try tightening it up to the ⅜" mark on the scale. If the blade still wanders, tighten it up a little more. When you are satisfied, pluck the stationary blade and listen to its tone. If you have any musical inclination, you might even be able to identify the note. If you can, write it down for that size blade. Test for other sizes as well.

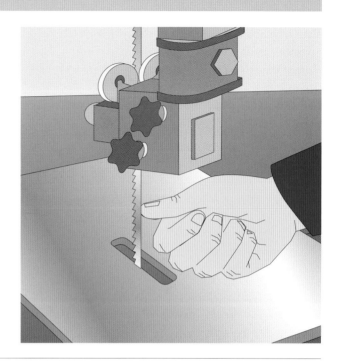

bar clamps, gripping

The conventional 6" to 12" bar clamps usually have smooth wooden screw handles on them. The manufacturers seem to forget that when someone works with wood, sawdust is created, and that sawdust will absorb the moisture in your hands. Therefore, when you try to tighten the handles, they slip. Here are two methods that will alleviate the problem. Locktite has a product called Color Guard. This is a liquid latex material that can be applied by dipping or brushing. It dries in about a half an hour. According to the manufacturer's instructions, two coats should be applied. Color Guard is available in half a dozen opaque colors as well as a clear application. It works very well.

bar clamps, gripping

Another method of improving your grip on wooden clamp handles is through the use of an old bicycle or car inner tire tube cut into strips. Or, plumbers use a rubber tape to temporarily stop water leaks. The tape sticks to itself and will help increase the grip on the clamp's handles.

battens, flexible

Battens made for the underside of edge-joined board tabletops must allow for the contraction and expansion of the table due to changing humidity conditions. To do this, route a groove down the center of the batten using a grooving bit with your router. Then rout an elongated holed in the groove in a couple of places. Screw the batten to the under part of the tabletop. Doing this will allow the tabletop to move.

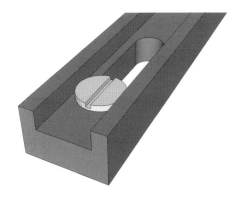

belt sander, safety guard

One of the handiest sanding machines that I have seen and used is the 1"-wide belt and 6" disc sander made by Delta. Its only weak spot is the opening at the top end of the belt rotation. This opening usually throws out a lot of sawdust directly at the user. To avoid this I made a curved shield out of scrap acrylic. I cut the piece to size and then used a heat gun to soften it and mold it to the shape I wanted. I used fiberglass reinforced tape to attach it to the tool. Should I want to use that portion of the sander, the new shield simply flips out of the way.

belt sander, longer belt life

Always loosen the pressure release on your belt sanders when they are idle; doing this will greatly extend the life of the belt. Better yet, remove the belt and store it on a pegboard nested with other belts of the same grit.

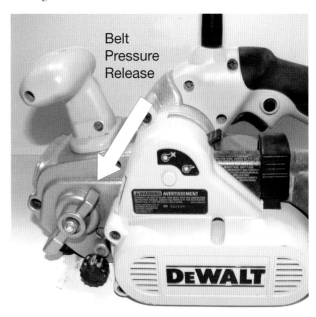

Belt Pressure Release

belt sander, storing belts

Store belt sander belts on a pegboard with belts of similar grits.

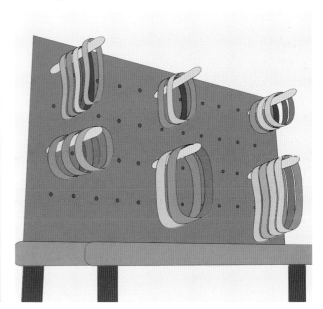

biscuits, storing

The biscuits used in biscuit joinery expand in the joint when glue is added, and that, in conjunction with the glue, helps to make a tight joint. The biscuits need to remain dry. Keep them in a sealed container with a pack of desiccant. Desiccant packs are used in electronics and camera shipping packages and if you talk nicely to your local camera dealer or electronic equipment dealer, they will probably give you a couple.

center punch, honing

A standard center punch is ground to a 60 degree point and this is fine for use with metalworking. For woodworking you are better off to re-grind the punch to a more acute angle. The sharper angle is better to start drill bits, centers for lathe headstocks, tailstocks, etc. To sharpen that center punch, mount the square end in a drill/driver and set the drill in reverse. Turn on your grinder and make your point while the drill is turning. You will get a far more accurate point on the tool by doing it this way.

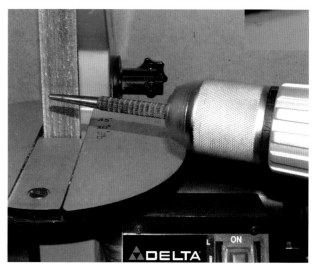

center punch, makeshift

If you don't have a center punch you can use a common drywall screw to mark your center.

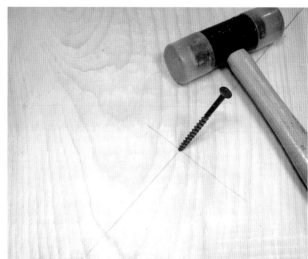

chisels, maintaining

Some of the better manufacturers of wood chisels suggest that you put an additional 2-degree edge on their chisels before using them. Don't stop there. When you are chiseling mortises, it is imperative that all sides are flat and parallel. This can be achieved only if the chisel backs are also flat. Verify this by laying the chisel blade flat on an oilstone and rubbing (lapping) it on the oilstone a few times. The high spots will show the grinding marks. If the gaps are serious, the blade will have to be flattened. Start with a coarse stone and work up to a fine stone until all the high spots are removed. Oh, one thing more. An often neglected area on chisels is the edges. Using the above method, check for high spots and grind them down as well.

circular saw, blade buying guide

One type of circular-saw blade is the carbide-tipped blade. This blade has a wide range of prices, and can be bought for as little as five dollars. It is much more durable than high-speed steel blades which are now rarely available. Purchase your blades from reputable dealers. Select only brand-name products.

One basic rule that should govern your blade selection is that the more teeth, the finer the cut. The number of teeth is proportionate to the size of the blade. For example, an 8" blade with 36 teeth will give about the same cut as a 10" blade with 50 teeth. Some blades, such as planer blades, tend to wobble slightly, and this will affect the cut. Therefore, a set of stabilizers is recommended. These stabilizers are like large washers that are slightly concave and fit on both sides of the blade to stabilize it.

There are also blades, generally 10" or 12" in diameter, which have a very shallow cutting sequence. These blades are very thin for the first 1½" or so, and then become thicker up to the arbor hole. They are meant for cutting thin materials such as plastic laminates, etc. There is a group of specialty blades that are designed to be used in particular woodworking situations. Included in this group are blades with 200 teeth that are used for plywood and give an extremely smooth cut. Unless you are in the woodworking business and set up for production, they probably won't concern you. Following are some types of blade that are recommended for use in the workshop. A combination blade is a general-purpose blade that will give fairly clean crosscuts and rip cuts. The more teeth it has, the finer the cut. A crosscut blade, as its name implies, is the blade best suited for crosscutting. It generally has more teeth to provide a smoother cross-grain cut. A planing blade gives an extremely smooth crosscut, but is very thin and should not be used for ripping or for very thick material. A rip blade generally has fewer teeth than other types of blade, because it faces less resistance as it is used to cut with the grain of the wood.

There are special blades for cutting plywood, plastics, laminates, particleboard, hardboard, nonferrous metals, etc. For information on these types of blades, consult a tool-shop specialist or mail-order catalogues.

circular saw, avoid tearout

Because the blade on a circular saw cuts "up", the tearout always occurs on the side the saw is resting on. Tear-out or ragged edges won't be a problem on your finished work if, when cutting with your circular saw, you make sure that the good side of your material is always facedown.

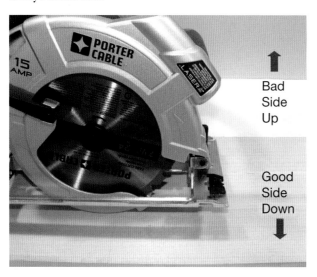

Bad
Side
Up

Good
Side
Down

circular saw, crosscut jig

Make your own custom crosscut circular saw guide for accurate cutting. This jig will guarantee perfectly square crosscuts every time. In addition, the kerf cut by the saw blade shows you precisely where to line up the jig.

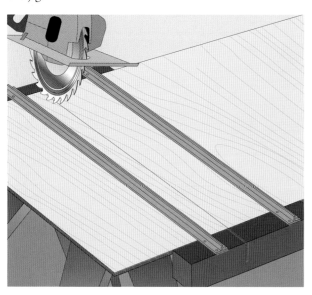

circular saw, cleaning blade

If your saw blades aren't cutting properly, it may be because the blade is dirty, not dull. Pine, spruce and other soft woods are the materials most likely to clog up a blade. They will leave a residue of tar and gum on your blades that will slow down the cutting rate or leave burn marks on your wood. They will also speed up the dulling process on the teeth. One method of cleaning is to spray on some oven cleaner. Let the oven cleaner remain on the blade for a couple of hours and then brush the blade clean. There are commercial blade cleaners available as well. Use the same cleaning methods for your other blades and bits.

circular saw, blade sharp?

The easiest way to determine whether or not your saw blades are sharp is to simply use your thumbnail on the tip of a randomly selected tooth. If the tooth leaves a scratch mark on your thumbnail, the blade is sharp. If it doesn't, have it sharpened. Never use a dull saw blade. Dull blades can cause excessive strain on your saw's motor and severely shorten its life.

circular saw, fitting blades

If you have a circular saw blade with an arbor hole that is too big for the saw arbor, don't throw it away. Most hardware or tool stores carry reducing washers for just this purpose.

circular saw, straightedge guide

When using a straightedge as a guide for ripping with your portable circular saw, you usually have to add the distance from the blade to the edge of the saw shoe to your measurements. If you are a weekend wood-worker, you probably have to verify this measurement with a measuring tape each time you use the saw. To save some time when you next use the saw, write the measurements from both sides of the blade to the shoe edges on the motor housing of your saw. Write these measurements on a sticky label or use a soft-tip marker. Most saw blades cut a ⅛" kerf, but make a test cut with your blade and add its kerf measurement on the motor housing with the other measurements.

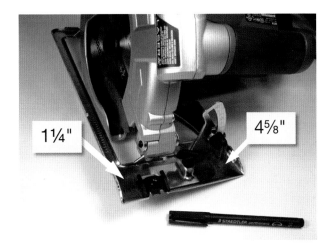

1¼"   4⅝"

circular saw, zero-clearance base

Your circular saw will almost always leave tear-out when cutting plywood because the leading edge of the saw blade cuts up from under the sheet. You can reduce that tear-out on the face or good side of the plywood by having the good side on the bottom. You can really reduce tear-out by fitting a sub-base of Masonite to your saw. Use double-face tape to adhere it. Raise the blade, adhere the sub-base and then lower the blade through it. Be very careful however, the blade guard will not function with this sub-base attached.

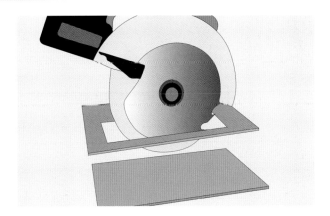

circular saw, storing blades

Many circular-saw blades are packaged in a plastic container. Save these containers. They are very handy for cleaning blades. They may also be available without a blade at some woodworking supply retailers.

clamping aids

There is a simple technique that will help you hold a project with one hand, slip a piece of scrap wood into the clamp jaws, and tighten the clamp all at the same time. Simply use double-faced tape on the wood scraps to adhere them to the clamp jaws. Double-faced tape can be found at art supply houses or carpet dealers.

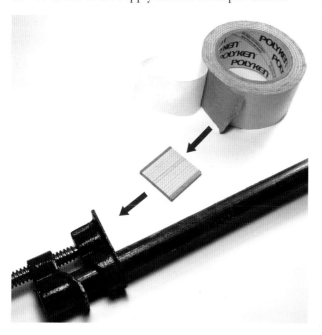

circular saw, storing blades

The simple storage cabinet shown below was built to store all my 10" circular saw blades. The shelves are made of scrap ³⁄₁₆" paneling, while the top, sides and bottom are made of ¾" plywood. When putting my blades away, I slip a piece of Styrofoam packing or bubble wrap underneath the blade. Never allow blades to come into contact with each other when storing them. Carbide-tooth tips can be very brittle.

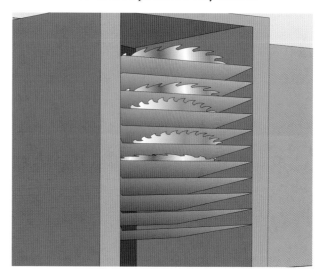

clamps, clothespins

Looking for a clamp to hold that small project while the glue is drying? Check the laundry room. A spring clothespin is ideal for just this kind of situation.

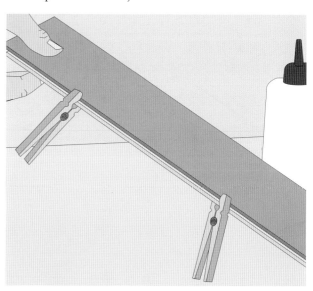

clamps, edging

Edge clamping is sometimes difficult if you don't have those special edge clamps. You can solve that problem by using conventional short bar or 'C' clamps. Tightly (with protection pads) clamp the table surface and then use wooden shims between the clamp body and the table edge, pushing them tightly.

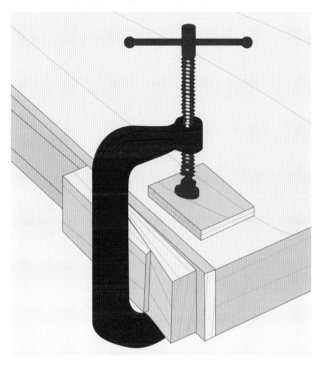

clamps, odd shapes

Nylon tie wraps can be used in lieu of a strap clamp for clamping odd-shaped workpieces. Link them together and then pull them all tight.

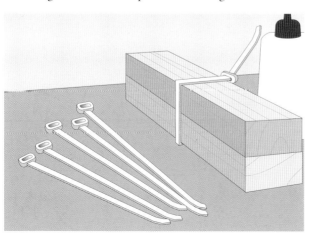

clamps, emergency

Need one more clamp? Maybe a caulking gun will help. It may be crude, but it will work in some circumstances.

clamps, pipe

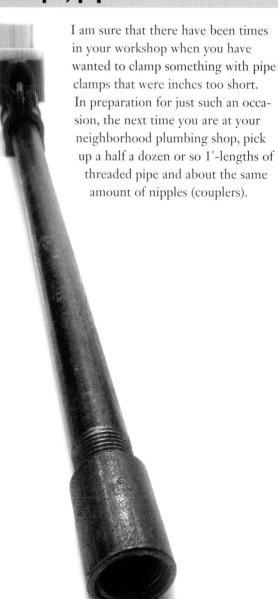

I am sure that there have been times in your workshop when you have wanted to clamp something with pipe clamps that were inches too short. In preparation for just such an occasion, the next time you are at your neighborhood plumbing shop, pick up a half a dozen or so 1'-lengths of threaded pipe and about the same amount of nipples (couplers).

127

clamps, protecting work

To prevent a bar or 'C' clamp from marring your workpiece use the cap from a soda bottle on the screw end. Cut a piece out of the top of the cap to fit the fixed end.

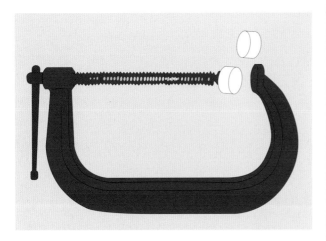

clamps, protecting work

Here's a new twist on how to protect your workpiece when gluing it up. Save the plastic caps from plastic prescription bottles. The caps make great pads for clamps. Sometimes the supplied pads get misplaced so these caps will come in handy. There are a number of ways that you can apply them to the clamps. The easiest would be to use thin-foam double-faced tape.

clamps, protecting work

The pipe in pipe clamps can leave stains on the workpiece. To prevent this, wrap short lengths of foam pipe insulation around the pipe to keep it off the surface of the project.

clamps, protecting work

To prevent bar or pipe clamps from marring your workpieces make a series of clamp pads and keep them handy. Using a router, with a ¾" bit, route a 3"-long groove into scrap softwood as shown.

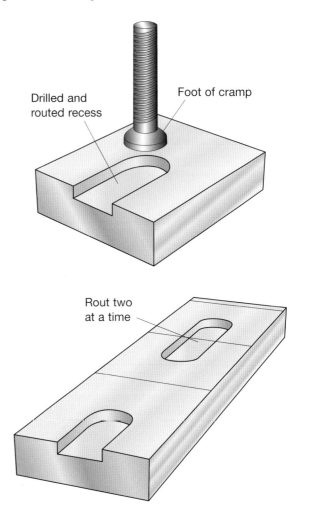

Drilled and routed recess

Foot of cramp

Rout two at a time

clamps, protecting work

Felt furniture foot pads make excellent clamp pads. They are available in various sizes and are adhesive-backed so they will stay on your clamps.

clamps, shop-made

Four blocks of hardwood scraps such as maple or oak and some hooks are virtually all that is needed to make the framing clamps shown here. After they are made and the hooks are in place, go out to your car roof rack or into your camping gear and pick out one long or four equal-sized bungee cords. If using four equal-sized pieces of cord, connect each piece to a hook and attach the hook to one of the blocks of hardwood. There you have it.

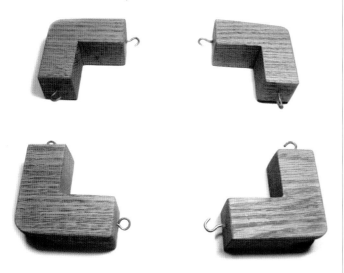

clamps, rubber band

Stationary supply stores carry a wide range of elastic bands and these make perfect clamps for odd sizes of workpieces. You can usually purchase a variety pack of different sizes. Keep them handy as you'll find many other uses for them as well.

clamps, shop-made

Make your own framing clamps easily and inexpensively by using four cabinet strap hinges. First, bend the tails back to 90 degrees. Next, drill holes in the tails to facilitate ³⁄₁₆" or ¼" threaded rod. Use washers and wing nuts on the threaded rod.

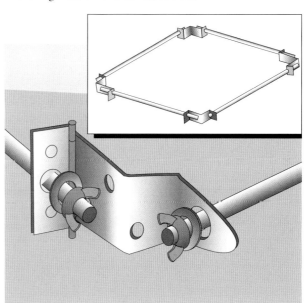

clamps, shop-made

Got a bicycle that's building up a coat of rust in the back of your garage? I thought so. Remove the tires and pull off the inner tubes. Make two crosscuts, one on either side of the valve stem. Now, with a pair of sharp scissors, start to make a continuous cut, about an inch wide. Do this through the entire length of the tubes. You now have a handy clamp. When gluing up projects such as chair legs and rungs, wrap the rubber-band clamp around the workpiece a couple of times and tie it tight. An added benefit: Take the rubber bands with you next time you go to the lumberyard. They are great for tying material to your car's roof rack.

clamps, storage

Sometimes the clamps that you need for that glue up project are on the other end of your workshop. Here's a convenient way of keeping them closer to your work. Cut some short lengths of PVC (polyvinyl chloride) or ABS (acrylonitrile-butadiene-styrene) pipe and put them in one of those old plastic buckets. Place your clamps into the pipe tubes. The bucket makes it easy to move the clamps to the workplace. You could also place the bucket on a wheeled dolly for easier portability.

clamps, storage

Bar clamps can be stored on hooks on a pegboard, but they take up a lot of room. The method described here is more efficient. I have found a nook in my shop for a shop-made rack. Using aluminum angle, I drilled holes in one side of the rack and then cut into the holes to make slots. The angle was mounted on a board and the board was screwed into the concrete wall, I can get 29 clamps in a 40"-length of angle.

clamps, strap

A nylon-web hold-down strap, available at automotive accessory dealers or truck rentals, is the ideal clamp to use for gluing veneer edges to a round surface such as a tabletop. The web strap is also a great clamp for use on loosened chair rungs and legs.

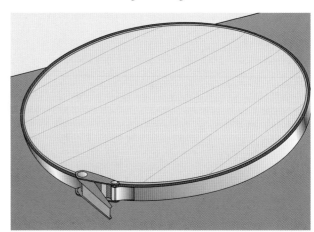

clamps, tie wraps

A broken chair leg or arm spindle is sometimes difficult to clamp until the glue sets. There are a number of ways to do it, but in most cases the clamp ends up sticking to the workpiece after the glue has dried. One way to prevent this is to use tie wraps instead. Keep a number of tie wraps in different sizes on hand for such occasions. The tie wraps are made of a nylon material and won't stick after the glue has dried. A pair of wire cutters is all that's needed for removal. Tie wraps are available at most hardware stores, probably in their electrical department.

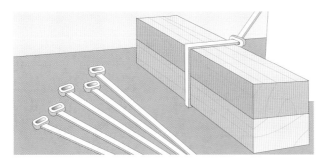

depth gauge, shop-made

A simple but efficient depth gauge for setting table-saw blade heights or router-bit depths can be made from either a hex bolt, a carriage bolt or a length of threaded rod. Two nuts can be used, one to set the depth and the other to lock it.

coping saw jig

The coping saw-also referred to as a fretsaw is used for fine and delicate cutting of the softer woods. The shop-built coping saw jig shown is easy to make and an indispensable tool if you are doing any fretsaw work.

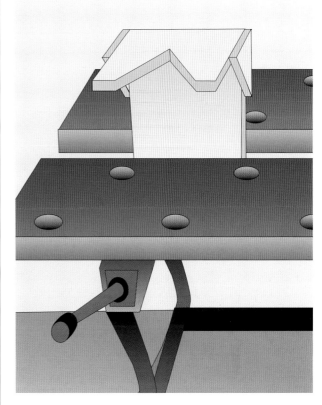

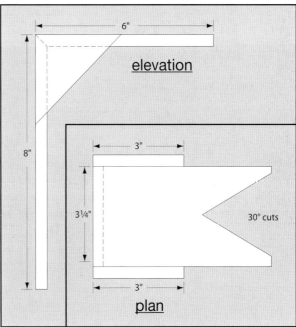

elevation

6"

8"

3"

3¼"

30° cuts

3"

plan

drill bits

There are a variety of drill bits available that will prove helpful to woodworkers:

BRAD-POINT (A) bits have a spur on their tips to prevent wandering, especially on odd shapes.

EXPANSIVE (B) bits are an adjustable form of spade bit with adjustments in ¹⁄₁₆" to a maximum of 1¼".

HIGH-SPEED-STEEL (HSS) (C) bits are general purpose bits that may be used on both wood and metal.

SELF-FEED (D) bits are used for aggressive drilling of larger holes in heavy wood stock. The self–feed bits are mostly used in residential construction.

AROUND-THE-CORNER (E) bits are a type of spade bit used in construction and can actually drill a curved or "S" type hole in wood.

CONCRETE (F) drill bits are used for drilling into concrete and have a carbide tip.

SHIP AUGER (G) bits are very aggressive wood bits with larger diameters and longer lengths.

SPADE (H) bits are used for rough drilling of holes from ¼" to 2" diameter.

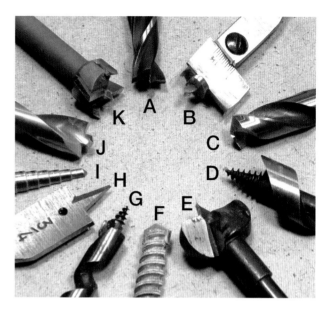

STEP (I) bits are available in a variety of diameters and step heights and are mainly used for drilling into sheet metal.

MODIFIED BRAD-POINT (J) bits are titanium-coated and stay sharp longer.

FORSTNER (K) bits are available in high-speed steel and carbide steel. They drill a clean hole and leave a flat bottomed hole.

drill bits, cleaning

Drill bits tend to accumulate a buildup of tar and gum after extended use. To remove this residue, soak them for approximately 15 minutes in a solution of washing soda and water. Use an old toothbrush to scrub them clean. Wipe them dry.

drill bits, truing

The tip of a high-speed-steel drill bit is set at a particular angle for the most efficient cutting. Sometimes after sharpening, whether you do it yourself or have it done professionally, you may want to verify the point angle. The following technique will make it simple: Go to your parts bins and pick out a couple of hex nuts, place them side by side. The tip of the bit should fit between the two nuts without any visible air space.

DRILL PRESSES

The drill press makes an effective workshop companion and is found in many workshops. Although its primary purpose is to drill holes, it can be used for other operations. The drill press is often thought of as a simple woodworking machine to use and, as a result, a lot of users take it for granted. The drill press, like any piece of machinery, is a dangerous tool if safety precautions are not followed. You should securely clamp all work to be drilled, wear safety goggles and be sure that you are using the correct speed for the type of drill bit or other equipment that you have installed. It is important to remember that a drill press does not have a brake on it and the spindle will continue to rotate for a moment or two after turning it off.

drill press, angle jigs

Drilling a 30-degree hole in a small workpiece takes a lot of time, even when you have an auxiliary table attached to your drill press. A lot of us lazy people look at what's involved and then resort to the portable drill and hope for the best. Here's an easier way: Build yourself a set of ramps, six in all. Build them at 15, 20, 22.5, 25, 30 and 45 degrees. Drill holes in them and hang them up on a pegboard located near your drill press. You'll find that this will be a real time saver for those angled holes.

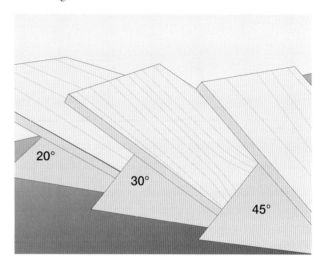

drill press, auxilliary table

I made the auxiliary table for my drill press shown here out of ¾" plywood and securely bolted it to the drill press table with carriage bolts, washers and wing nuts. Wing nuts make it easy to remove if I want to do any metal drilling. I can also leave it in place and put another surface under the metal workpiece. I made my table 24" wide, but you can make yours to whatever size is needed. The adjustable fence shown is made from 2"-square aluminum tubing and strap steel that is 1" wide and ⅛" thick. Although the fence fits tightly, I still use clamps to make sure that it doesn't move when I'm using it. I also make sure that it is square to the table before clamping it.

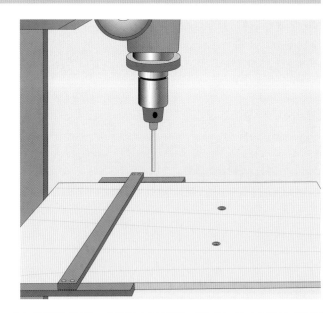

drill press, chuck key store

The chuck key for a drill press can often be difficult to locate. To make sure that the chuck key will not be misplaced, attach a rare-earth magnet to the upper housing of the drill press. This will secure the chuck key and keep it handy.

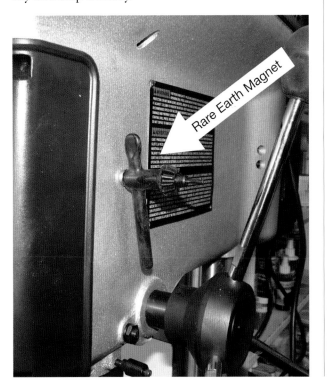

Rare Earth Magnet

drill press, circle-cutter safe

Circle cutters, sometimes known as fly cutters, can be downright dangerous to use. The arm and the bit are rotating at high speeds and it is difficult to see them. To make them more visible, I painted the ends a bright fluorescent yellow. It helps.

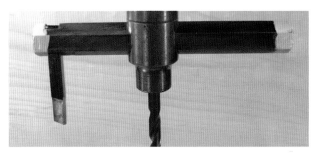

drill press, depth gauge

Do your kids play with Lego® building blocks? Use the thin ones as a depth gauge for your drill press or table saw. The thin building blocks are exactly ⅛" in thickness if they are the Lego brand. Build those Lego blocks into a stair configuration so that you will have ⅛" graduations for many tool setting operations. You may have to glue them together with a plastic adhesive.

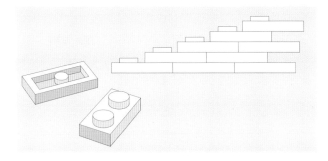

drill press, drilling dowels

The photo shows a simple jig for drilling into the ends of dowels that can be clamped onto a drill press table. To make this jig, take stock 1×4×8", find its center along its length and drill a hole the same diameter as the dowel. A forstner bit will provide a cleaner hole. Drill the hole through the stock. After you have marked the center of your dowel end, fit it into the hole and drill it.

drill press, drilling dowels

Take a piece of wood 2" wide × 2" thick × about 12" long and rip a V down the middle of it on your table saw. Drill a ¼" hole into one end. You have made a simple jig for drilling holes into the edge of a dowel, round chair leg, etc. The hole is used to hang the jig on the pegboard right next to the drill press.

drill press, drilling dowels

Drilling into the ends of dowels can be made more accurate by notching a V into your hand screw. Cut the notch with your band saw.

drill press, drilling into spheres

Wooden balls or spheres are used a lot in toy making and don't usually come pre-drilled. To drill them precisely through the middle can be very frustrating and wasteful. Here's a technique that works for me: Let's say you have a 2"-diameter wooden ball that you want to drill through. Clamp a piece of ¾"-thick scrap to your drill-press table and, using a Forstner or a spade bit, drill a 1" hole part way through the stock. Remove the bit, but do not move the stock or reset the drill press. Now, install the desired size of drill bit into the chuck, place the ball in the hole, and drill. By preventing movement of the scrap piece you are assured of drilling into the middle of the sphere.

drill press, lathe

A drill press can be used as a lathe for simpler jobs when a lathe is not available. Using ½" × 3" hardwood stock, cut an L-shape with a tail on it. The tail is for firmly clamping the piece to the drill-press table. A gusset is glued and screwed to the upright for stability, and the upright may be used as a tool rest. The base of the L-shaped piece becomes the lathe tailstock. Holes are centered on the base to accommodate pointed dowel markers. The headstock is the appropriately sized Forstner drill bit. The three important things to be done are to make sure that the middle of the stock will rotate, the tailstock is regularly oiled, and the drill press is operated at a slow speed. Extreme care should be used during this operation and all safety measures should be adhered to.

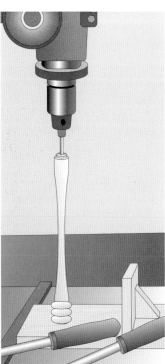

drill press, marking work

When drilling into a finished workpiece you probably don't want to mark it up with X pencil lines to show where to drill holes. Make your X on a sticky note and place that on it. The sticky note won't leave any residue to mar the finished piece.

drill press, sanding wheels

If you are into toy-making, this technique will expedite the process if your toys require wheels. After your wheels are cut, insert a hex bolt of the required length and diameter through the centers. Use a flat washer between each wheel. Next, lock them on tight with a hex nut, being sure to place a washer between the bolt and the last wheel. Insert the tail end into the chuck of your drill press and tighten it. Turn your drill press on to a medium speed. A strip of sandpaper is all that is required to round off the edges. The washers allow you to get between the wheels so that you can do all of the edges in one operation.

drill press, stop

Your builders' square is the perfect stop for drilling repetitive holes on your drill press. Clamp the two legs of the square to the drill press table and they will act as both the stop and a fence. Care must be taken to blow away or vacuum the chips between drilling.

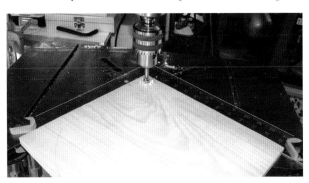

drill press, setting table angle

The drill press angle jigs described earlier can also be used to set the angle of your drill-press table if you prefer. The method is simple. Loosen the adjustment screws on the table, set a level on the required angle jig so that it is horizontal and tighten up the screws.

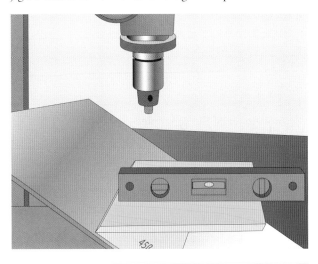

drill press, tightening bits

After removing a drill bit from your drill press, if you notice some scraping of the bit shank take another look at how you installed the bit. The scraping of the shank is usually caused by a loose chuck; the bit is losing its grip. To prevent this, make it a habit to tighten all three holes in the drill chuck.

drill press, truing up table

A drill press will not be effective if the
chuck is not perfectly perpendicular
to the table (unless, of course, you are
angle-drilling). An easy way to true up
your table is to do the following: Take
a wire coat hanger, a piece of aluminum
rod or any scrap metal rod and make two
90-degree bends in it so that it is shaped
like a Z. Then tighten one end into your
chuck. Do not turn your drill press on.
Lower the shaft until the coat hanger just
touches the table. Now, lock the shaft and
slowly hand-turn the chuck. If you see
a gap between the table and the hanger,
adjust your table accordingly.

dust collection, air cleaners

Shop air cleaners are really efficient in
removing floating sawdust from your
shop. They are noisy in home workshops
because they are usually suspended from
the overhead joists and when turned on
they reverberate through the floor above.
To avoid this, hang the unit with large
rubber 0 rings, heavy-duty nylon tie wraps
or even strong springs, between the air-
cleaner hooks and the support hooks.
These will dampen the vibration and
reduce the noise in your living space.

dust collection, clearing sawdust blockage

If you are using ABS or PVC piping for your central
sawdust collection unit, here is a way to ensure that
any clogging of the pipes can be readily cleared. Most
fittings such as elbows, "Ts," "Y"s and connectors fit
tightly without the use of a solvent glue. Leave them
just that way. There will be very little air or pressure
loss and you will be thankful if there is a blockage in
the line.

dust collection, clearing sawdust blockage

Flexible hoses can be easily dismantled because of the screw-type fastening clamps. However, you should not make the runs too long. You may have to get inside them for clean out. There is a 4" flexible hose made of a clear plastic material that will easily show you where the blockage is located.

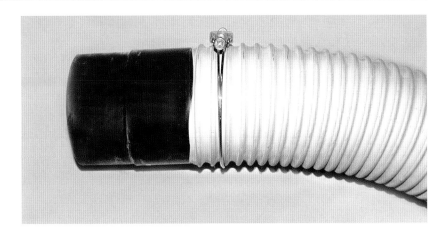

dust collection, down draft

A down-draft table is a sanding table with a perforated top surface and a fan underneath that sucks the sawdust down and into a dust bag. It has the advantage of lowering the level of airborne sawdust. Down-draft sanding tables are quite expensive and generally made for commercial workshops. You can make your own on a smaller scale with pegboard. Build a frame of 1×4s about 12" wide × 24" long. Cut a slot around the perimeter to accommodate a piece of pegboard to fit. The slot should be about ¼" below the top edge. Cover the bottom of the frame with a solid piece of Masonite or thin plywood and then drill a hole in the center of one end to the size of your shop vacuum nozzle. To further improve the dust collection, use a countersink drill bit to chamfer each pegboard hole.

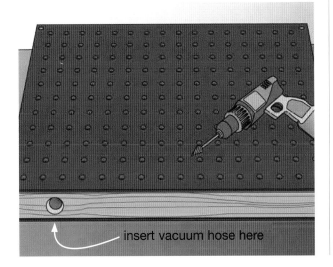

insert vacuum hose here

dust collection, collectors

Getting the metal strap around the lower dust bag of a dust collector can be frustrating. Using strong magnets like rare earth magnets can make the job easier. Place two or three around the bag and frame to hold the empty bag in place and then fasten the metal strap.

Rare Earth Magnets

dust collection, preventing blockage

When installing PVC rigid pipe for a central sawdust collection system, avoid the use of 90-degree elbows as these can quickly clog up — invariably they will.

Use "sweeps" which have a more gradual 90-degree turn. If these are not available, use two 45-degree elbows with a 3" length of pipe between them.

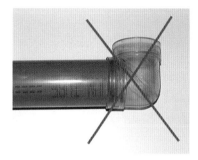 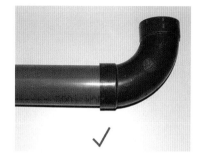 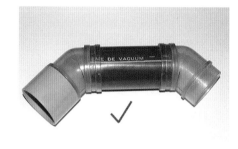

dust collection, portable tools

Most portable power tools made today have some sort of accommodation for the collection of sawdust. This is usually in the form of a tube near the rear of the tool; the sawdust is collected into a supplied cloth bag or a canister of sorts. The amount of sawdust collected is much less than 100 percent. Most of these tubes, though, are readily adaptable to shop vacuum cleaners, but that is not a sure thing. It seems there is no standard outlet size at this writing. There is an answer, however, and that is through the use of a heat gun. As these tubes are made of plastic, they can be reshaped to fit the nozzle of your shop vacuum quite easily. Some of the tubes are rectangular. A short length of PVC or ABS plastic pipe can be shaped to fit.

files, cleaning

Files and rasps tend to accumulate the materials you have tried to grind away in the crevasses of the tool. For some reason, aluminum builds up in a file and soon renders the file useless. Until now! Laying the file(s) in a warm solution of water and lye will quite quickly melt and eject any traces of aluminum. Be very careful when using lye. Wear thick rubber gloves, face and eye protection, and follow all safety instructions for use. This is very caustic material. If you spill any lye, immediately dilute it with water. After cleaning the file or rasp, rinse it well in cold water, wipe it dry and coat the tool with light oil.

files, making handles

Most files have sharp steel tangs that can be uncomfortable to use. Old ballpoint pens with the ink tube removed can be used for handles on these files. A heat gun will soften the plastic to mold onto the tang.

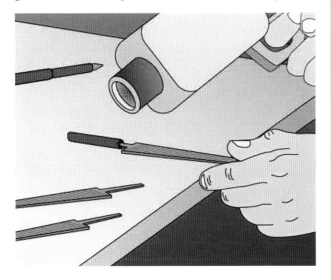

filters, disposable

Don't throwaway that paper dust mask just yet: It can be reused. Simply vacuum the outside surface and then use it for filtering paint thinners or other lightweight liquids. If the dust mask remains clean and the product it was used to filter was clear, the dust mask can be reused as a filter.

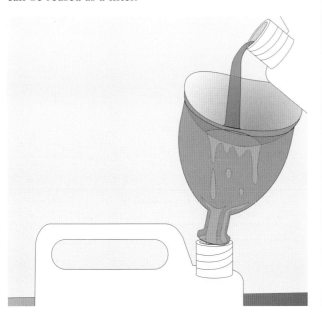

files, making handles

Another approach taken by many woodworkers is to turn their own wooden handles on their lathe, and then drill out for the tang and make a slice (kerf) across the end. This is done so that some sort of binding can be wrapped around the end to tightly secure the file on the handle. Ferrules can serve as this binding. Ferrules can be found at your local plumbing supply store. Ask for copper pipe end caps. These can be drilled and filed to fit the tang and then force fitted over the end of the turned handle.

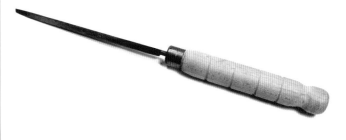

hammer, new handle

A wooden hammer handle can get pretty slippery after many years of use. Most woodworkers have their favorite hammer and they hate to give it up even if unsafe. To renew the grip of the wooden hammer handle, use a countersink bit to drill dimples into the grip portion. A little sanding and you will get a better grip on it.

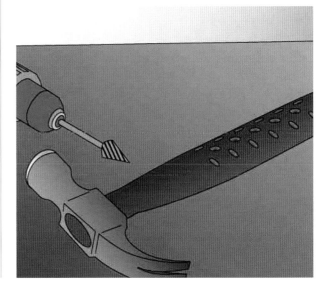

handsaw, japanese

The Japanese handsaw, usually referred to as a dozuki saw, is much different from the traditional back or tenon saw. In the traditional saws, the teeth are set in a crosscut configuration and are meant to cut on the push stroke. Because of the pushing action, the blades must be very rigid, and therefore must be thick. The Dozuki saw, on the other hand, has teeth that are set to cut on the pull stroke. This results in a more accurate cut. Also, because of the pulling action, thinner steel is required, resulting in a narrower kerf. The finer steel allows for the finer cutting of the teeth. The traditional dozuki saw has 22 to 26 teeth per inch (tpi). Dozuki saws are now readily available in most home renovation stores. Generally, the blades of these saws are not meant to be re-sharpened; they are disposable. However, when dull they can be used as glue spreaders or scrapers.

hand tools, cleaning

A bench-type belt sander will help to take dirt and goo off tools like awls, knives, putty knives and chisels. An inverted portable belt sander clamped in your bench vise will work as well. Be careful not to leave the tools on the sanders too long as they could heat up and destroy the temper of the cutting edges.

handsaw, shop-made

Often, I have required the use of a small, fine-toothed saw to clean out cuts that are in tight locations. A hacksaw blade would sometimes suffice, but then I thought of using a jigsaw blade. I started with a ¾" dowel for the handle and cut a slot in the end with the band saw. I then drilled two small holes in the handle like the ones on the tail of the jigsaw blades. I flared the holes with a countersink, put the blade into the slot and installed the blade with a couple of No. 4 × ⅝" wood screws.

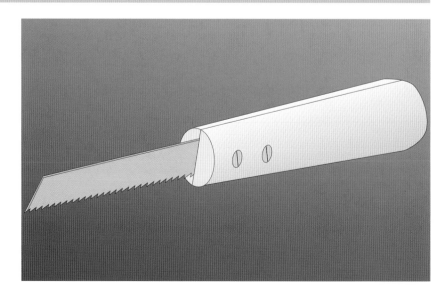

hand tools, covers

A length of old garden hose can come in handy in the woodshop. Cut short pieces of it to cover the jaws of tools like Vise-Grips and slip-joint pliers to protect your projects. If necessary, slice the pieces laterally to fit.

hand tools, mending handles

One way of mending the handles of your hand tools is by dipping them in a product called Color Guard, made by Locktite. This is a thick, liquid, rubbery material that semi-hardens. It softens the grip on the tools. Color Guard is available in about six colors, so it makes tools easily identifiable.

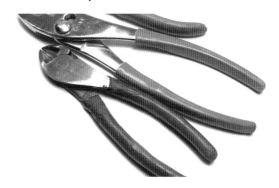

hand tools, mending handles

Hand tools, like pliers, wire cutters, etc., are bought with plastic-coated or rubberized grips. After a lot of use, these grips either break or wear off. Here's an easy way to mend them. Cut heat-shrink tubing, available by the length at most electrical supply shops in various colors and sizes, to the size of your particular handle(s). Now, keep a hair dryer or a heat gun nearby, ready for use. Coat the handle(s) with contact cement, and, while the glue is still wet, slip on the heat-shrink tubing and shrink the tubing with the hair dryer. The result is new handle grips.

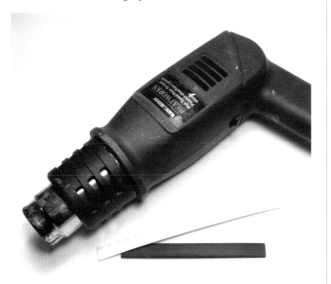

hand tools, preserving

You can preserve your hand tools and keep them rust-free by using a product called Rust Check, which prevents rust from forming. It is available from auto parts dealers in an aerosol can so it makes Rust Check easy to apply. To use it, soak your (metal) hand tools in it for a day or so and then wipe them off. Repeat this process once a year.

hand tools, preserving

When storing your favorite hand plane, use flat magnet-sign material to cover the exposed blade to save it from damage. The material is usually available from plastics dealers.

hand tools, protecting edges

Tools like chisels have very sharp edges and carrying them in a tool bag can either cut you or damage the edge of the tool. Foam pipe insulation wrapped around the blade will protect both.

hand tools, protecting edges

Spot-glue some indoor/outdoor carpet remnants to the bottoms of your tool-cabinet drawers. It will stop your tools from bouncing around and rattling if your toolbox is being transported.

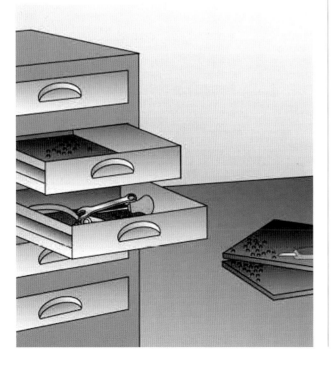

hacksaw, blade installation

There is some debate as to which way to install a hacksaw blade, should the teeth face forward or backward? The answer is most definitely, forward. For proof, take a look at other metal cutting blades like those for a jig saw and a reciprocal saw and that should convince you.

hole saws, enlarging holes

To enlarge a hole already made with a hole saw, try this. Cut a square piece of Masonite or thin plywood and make an X on it to find the center. Use the existing hole saw to penetrate the square with the pilot bit just enough to "scratch" it with the outer blade to show the diameter. Flip the piece over, insert the hole saw and use the bit to line up the piece, then nail it down. Install the larger cutter. Drill from the side opposite the Masonite. Hole saws are always easier to use in a drill press. They do not tend to wander or kick back.

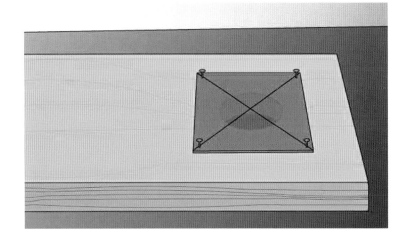

hole saw, increasing cutting depth

The usual cutting depth of a hole saw is 1$\frac{9}{16}$". To double the cutting depth, extend the length of the pilot bit or use a longer drill bit so that the bit will penetrate through the thicker piece. Once the bit has poked through, use the hole saw from the other side. You should now be able to cut to a depth of 3$\frac{1}{8}$".

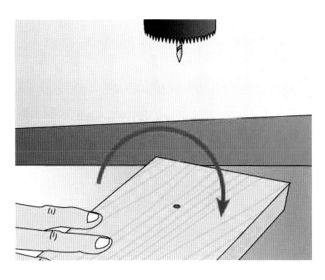

hole saw, making rings

There are a number of ways to make rings of different diameters, but the easiest that I have found is to "double stack" a couple of hole saws. Say, for example, you want a ½"-thick ring that is 2" on the outside and 1½" on the inside. Take your hole-saw mandrel and put a 2⅛" hole saw bit on it along with a 1½" bit. The ⅛" difference is to compensate for the blade thickness. Line them up in the mandrel, tighten the nut and proceed to drill on the drill press. When finished, disassemble the saws and you will have your ring. A number of combinations of hole-saw sizes may be used in this manner as long as the hole saws will fit onto the mandrel and the mandrel nut is secure.

hole saws, releasing plugs

Spray the inside and the outside of the hole saw with silicone or cooking spray. Then drill about three-quarters of the way into the stock or until the pilot bit goes right through the stock. Flip the workpiece over and drill from the other side. You will find that the plug will then drop out of the hole saw quite easily and will not be marred, as would happen if you attempted to pry it out. A word of caution however, if you plan to stain or clear coat the interior walls of the hole or the plug, don't use the spray.

hole saws, releasing plugs

If the plug is really stuck in the hole saw: Remove the saw from the drill press, unscrew the mandrel nut and gently tap the mandrel out. The plug should come out with it. All that's left to do is "unscrew" the plug off the pilot bit.

jigsaw, blade storage

A magnetic kitchen-knife holder will hold your jigsaw and reciprocal saw blades.

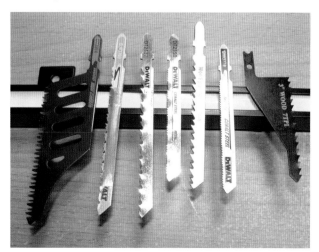

jointer, fixing nicks in knives

A nick in a jointer knife blade can ruin a joining operation; it will leave a raised stripe on the board you are
dimensioning. A quick fix before re-sharpening all of
the knives is to slightly shift one of the knives to the
left or the right. The nick will then cancel out.

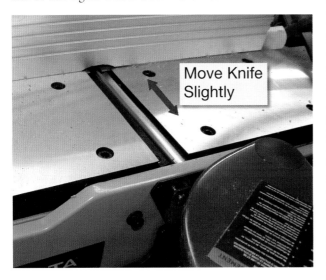

Move Knife
Slightly

lathe, clearing chips

Cleaning up after a day of lathe turning can be a
pain in the you-know-where. In fact, the worst part
of the clean-up is the shavings that collect under and
between the bed rails. When I'm bowl turning, I have
a length of ⅛" MDF that I lay over the rails to keep
the chips where they belong; on the floor.

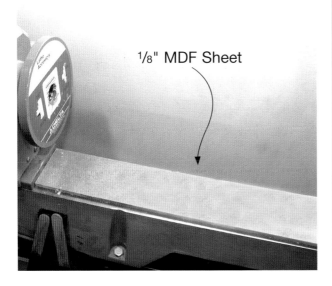

⅛" MDF Sheet

lathe, prolonging life

Most wood turners whom I have seen set up their
workpiece right on the lathe. They either tap the piece
into the headstock spur or they force it in by screwing
in the tailstock. The problem with doing it this way
is the jolts put pressure on the motor bearings. This
will shorten the life of even the best of lathes. On
your next wood-turning project, try this: Remove the
spur from the headstock and tap the spur into the end
of the workpiece with a wooden mallet. Once your
marks are made and the cut is deep enough, put the
spur back in the headstock and then tighten up the
tailstock. You will find that a lot less pressure is put on
the motor.

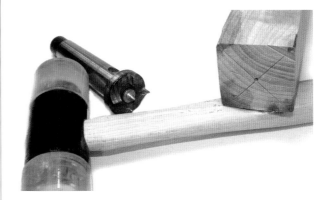

lathe, marking

Marking an X on dark wood can be made much clear-
er using White-Out on the end grain. Some White-
Out is available as a pen so you can use it to make
your X. Or, if you use the brush-on type, let it dry and
use a pencil to make your mark.

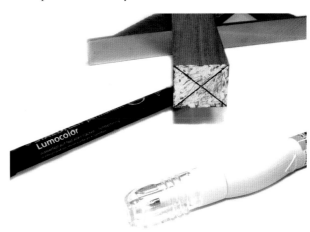

lathe, sanding with

Sanding your workpiece on the lathe while it is turning is an efficient way of getting a smooth finish. However, it has its drawbacks. The sandpaper can get pretty hot, sometimes too hot. The jig shown here is a shop-made tool that allows you to sand a workpiece on a lathe without heating the sandpaper. It takes about half an hour to make, and is made from 1"-thick hardwood or two pieces of ½"-thick plywood glued together. The tool uses 1"-wide sanding strips that are sold in rolls of varying lengths and grits. The strips are held in the slots with small wedges. If you plan it right, you can turn the strip end over end to make use of the unused portion. After you have determined the length of the sanding strip and cut it, cut several others of various grits to save time later.

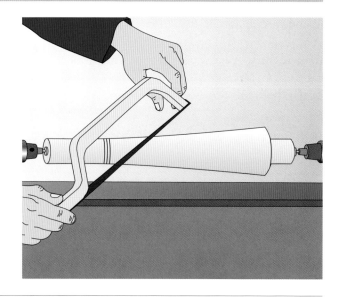

lathe, shop-made sanding drums

There are two ways that I know of to make a long sanding drum that fits on your lathe. The first is to turn the drum using a piece of softwood of the desired length. The diameter of the drum is also optional, but 2" is a handy size. First, apply a coat of contact cement to the dowel. Then apply contact cement to the back of a roll of 1"-wide sanding strips; the grit size of the sanding strips is up to you. Start applying the sanding roll to the dowel on an angle (10 to 15 degrees is fine). When done, trim off the ends. Be certain to make a mark where the headstock end will be. In the second method, make or buy a dowel, but divide it in three. Apply a coarse sanding strip on the left, a medium in the middle and a fine strip on the right. Pieces of tape with the various grits written on them will divide the sections. This will improve the drum's versatility and save you the time of changing drums.

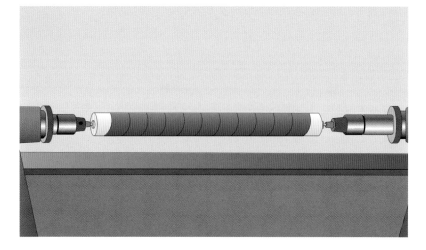

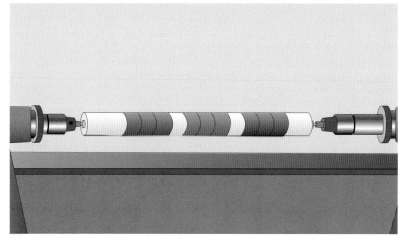

marking knife, making

Woodworkers always show their pride in home- or shop-made tools. Here is a way to make your own marking knife. Turn the handle from an exotic hardwood scrap. Make the blade from a worn-out hacksaw blade. It is best to grind grooves across the blade to make it easier to snap off the piece you want. Grind the blade to the desired shape. Cut a groove in the handle to fit the blade and use epoxy to keep it in place.

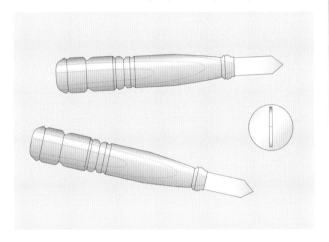

miter gauge, better grip

Your miter gauge will better grip the workpiece if you adhere a piece of emery cloth or sandpaper to the face of the gauge with double-faced tape. It will prevent your workpiece from slipping while cutting or routing.

marking knife, makeshift

A makeshift marking gauge for a single specific job can be made with a piece of scrap wood and a drywall screw. Leave the head of the screw exposed the distance that you want to make your line and use the edge of the screw head to scribe the mark.

miter gauge, fitting

Occasionally, the miter gauge on your stationary power tools should be checked for snugness in the table slot. If you find that the gauge is loose, try the following: With the bar of the miter gauge on its side, place it in a steel vise or on a block of scrap hardwood. Take a pointed metal punch and peen the bar. Peening makes the steel of the bar expand and will therefore make the gauge fit tighter. It's best to tap the punch lightly at first and do it to both sides of the bar.

miter gauge, fitting

While we are on the subject of miter gauges, you may have noticed that the slots on your table saw or band saw are a little lower than the thickness of the bar. This sometimes makes the gauge "catch" on the edge when it is used with larger pieces of wood. Preventing this is easy: Simply grind or file a 45-degree angle on the edge of the metal saw table. This will ease the miter gauge up to the table level without disturbing your workpiece.

miter gauge, squaring

The screw-down pointer on your miter gauge can sometimes be knocked out of alignment if you happen to drop or hit the gauge. To ensure a true miter every time, check the accuracy of the miter gauge occasionally. The easiest way to ensure an accurate alignment is to turn the miter gauge upside down, loosen the adjusting knob, slide it into the groove on the tool table and press it against the table edge. Now, tighten the knob and adjust the pointer if necessary.

miter gauge, truing

Use a digital inclinometer to make certain that your miter gauge is accurate. Loosen the lock knob and

place the face on the edge of your table saw. Place the inclinometer on the table saw top and set it to '0' for verification. Use the magnet face of the inclinometer on the tongue of the miter gauge. The inclinometer should read 90 degrees. Adjust the miter gauge accordingly.

miter gauge, stop block

When making a stop block for your miter saw always miter the inside edge. This will insure that no sawdust will pile up and distort the block and the desired lengths of cut.

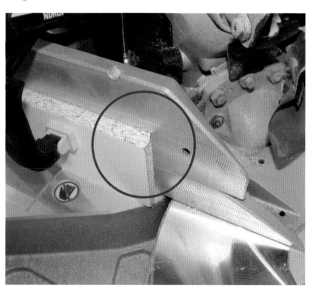

miter saw, space saving

Sliding compound miter saws are great but they take up a lot of space in a shop. Not so much the saw itself but the stock supports that one must have to hold those long pieces of wood. If your saw is in a fixed position against a wall we can save you some space. Fasten a couple of 2×4s to the wall and attach similar 2×4s with drop-down brackets and hinges to them. Adjust the height to match that of your saw table. You may want a couple of them on both sides of the saw.

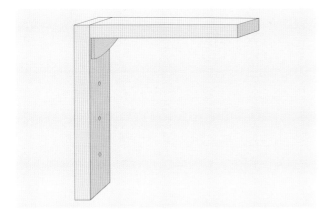

mobile base, small shops

Do you have a small shop? The best way to make use of every inch of floor space in a small shop is to mount your stationary tools on casters or mobile bases. There are a number of companies that make these and they are usually adaptable for almost any stationary tool.

miter saw, small pieces

Sometimes the opening between the fences of a compound miter saw is too wide to safely make a cut. The included clamp doesn't swing far enough either. So, to cut those smaller pieces here is the safe way of doing it. I made a clamping caul and that secures the small workpiece safely for cutting.

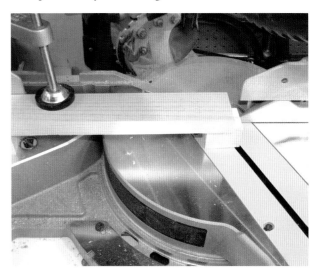

mortising machine, shims

There may be an occasion when mortises are required that are not at 90 degrees. Dedicated mortising machines usually don't allow you to vary the angle of the cut. Shims are the answer. For example, to offset the mortise cut by 5 degrees a simple shim of the same angle will work just fine.

5° Shim

pinch sticks

To make sure that your workpiece is square, use pinch sticks, or bar gauges. Component parts for pinch sticks are available at woodworking supply stores. Put the pinch sticks in the frame from corner to corner and tighten the lock screw. Measure the other diagonals and if there is a difference adjust the frame accordingly.

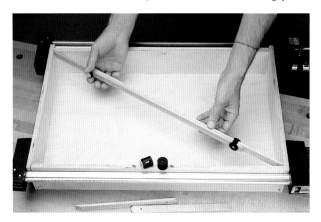

pinch sticks, temporary

Make your own pinch sticks from scraps as long as two pieces will fit in the diagonal of your frame. Use a strip of double faced tape or masking tape to hold the two pieces together when measuring one of the diagonals. If the sticks don't exactly fit in the other diagonal adjust the frame until it is square.

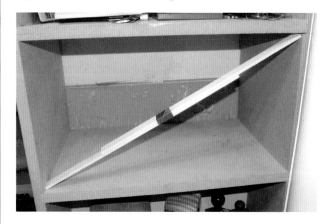

plane, block (protecting)

Keeping a block plane loose in a tool box will surely damage or nick the blade rendering the tool useless until re-ground and honed. Wrap your block plane in an old (or new) work glove to keep it safe until it is used.

pnuematics, compressor

Compact air compressors are now quite common in home workshops and they require regular maintenance to keep them working flawlessly and safely. The tank(s) should be drained on a regular basis to prevent internal rust. Spraying the inside of the tank of a new compact compressor with a rust preventative like RustCheck™ will extend the life of the air tank. To spray the interior, insert the plastic tube that comes with the spray can into the drain valve. Let the product sit for 24 hours and then drain it thoroughly. The air tank should be periodically checked externally for any signs of rust.

pneumatics, compressor

The compressor has an air filter to keep dust out of the piston chamber, and the filter should be checked and cleaned on a regular basis.

pneumatics, air nailer

After each use your air nailer or other air driven tool will really appreciate a little tender loving care. It won't take long but it will extend the life of the tools. Open up the nail chamber and blow it out with an air gun. Release the air jamb mechanism and blow that out as well. Use a Q-Tip™ dipped in compressor oil just to wipe in the nail chamber and in the jamb release area.

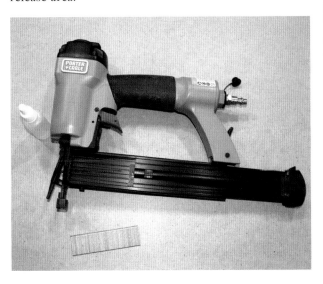

pneumatics, air nailer

Most of us woodworkers seem to neglect regular maintenance or our brad and finishing nailers as well as air staplers. They all need regular lubrication to lengthen their lives. We should make it a routine habit to put a drop or two of compressor oil into the compressed air fitting whenever you re-load with nails or staples.

pneumatics, hose storage

Keep your compressor air hose neatly tied by using hook and loop ties. Coil your air hose as you would normally do and then keep it that way with the hook and loop ties.

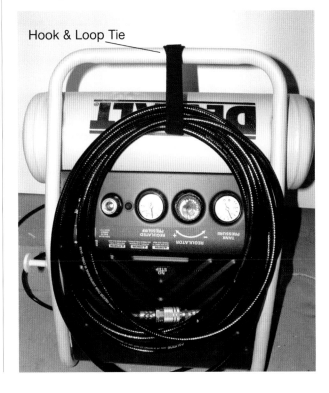

Hook & Loop Tie

153

pneumatics, longer hose

When using an air compressor) it is wiser to use long lengths of air hose to get to a remote work area rather than electrical extension cords. If you must use an extension cord, make sure that it has the correct rating. An incorrect wire gauge will put a strain on the electric motor and cause it to prematurely fail.

radial arm, cutting circles

You can make wheels or small, round tabletops on your radial arm saw. First, make as many angle cuts as you safely can, to get your workpiece close to round. Place your workpiece on the saw table so that it will clear the back fence. If you want an 18"-diameter table, for example, the radius will be 9". Therefore, measure 9" from the edge of the extended blade and about 10" out from the fence. Drill a nail through the center of the workpiece and into the saw table. Make sure it rotates freely. Now, holding the stock securely at the extreme left of the blade, start cutting a little bit at a time. Note: Do not attempt this procedure unless you are very familiar with the tool.

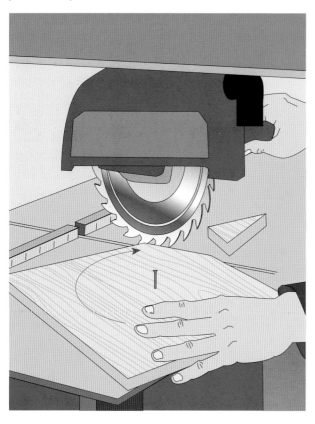

putty knife, honing

A quick and easy way to hone your scraper is the method shown here, using your random-orbital sander. Do this in short bursts, though, because you don't want to destroy the blade's temper.

radial arm, extension table

I soon realized that not only is an outfeed table a benefit, but so is an infeed table. However, both of these take up a lot of room and are not used all of the time. The solution then was to build a hinged in-feed table as shown here. When it's not in use it drops down out of the way. The fixed portion will easily handle 8' stock. I raise the hinged portion for longer stock and for sheets of plywood.

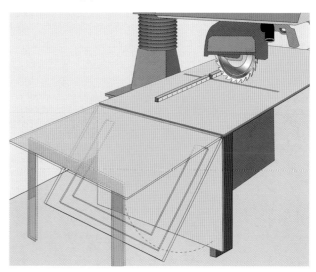

radial arm, stop block

The stop block shown here has been modified to increase its usefulness twofold. Rather than putting a T-nut in the middle of the block, as is normally done, I installed it closer to the bottom. By making this simple modification, the stop block can be raised, tightened, and used as a hold-down for ripping or for mitered cuts.

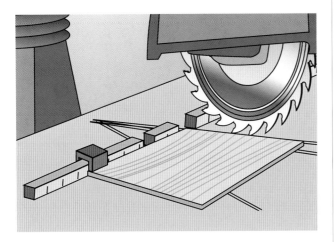

rasp, shop-made

Don't throwaway those old hacksaw blades. As a matter of fact, if you can scrounge some from your local friendly plumber, do so. A pile of them about 1½" thick will suffice. Make a stack and alternate the tooth direction of each blade. Install a nut and a bolt through the holes at each end and you have a really efficient rasp.

radial arm, stop block

When stop blocks are used for repetitive cuts the user should be aware that sawdust can accumulate in the corner and render the block inaccurate. Build a 2"-high × 6"-long × 2"-thick stop block out of scrap and cut 2" off the end. Fasten the two pieces together using a 2" butt hinge. To use the block, clamp the longer piece to your fence as required. Then, after each cut, swing the short end up to clear the table of sawdust.

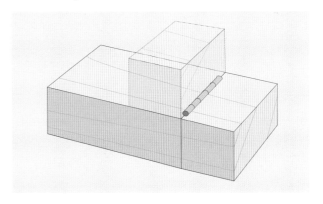

router, auxilliary base

Using your existing router base as a template, make two or three spare router bases out of ¼"-thick clear Plexiglas. Make the center hole of the bases slightly larger than your biggest bit. Round off the outer edges with a piece of fine sandpaper. A clear base makes freehand routing a lot easier because you can see much more of the surface you are working on. Leave the protective paper on the spare bases until you are ready to use them. Do not store the bases where direct sunlight will come into contact with them.

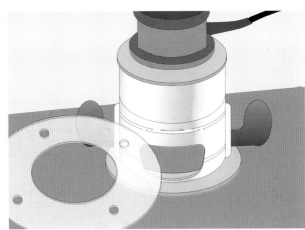

router, base (measuring)

Measure the diameter of your router base plate. Write this distance with a soft-tip marker on a sticky label and adhere it to the motor housing for future reference. This will save repeated measurements later.

router, bit installation

There is a correct and a safe way to install a bit in your router. Open the collet and insert the router bit until it hits bottom. Now, raise the router bit about ⅛" and securely tighten the collet. This will make removal easier when the job is done.

router, baseboards

Refinishing a room? If the job includes installing new baseboards, do a little modification to them first. Set up your router table with a rabbeting bit and route a ½" groove on the bottom of the back face. It can be used for running speaker wires or extension cords.

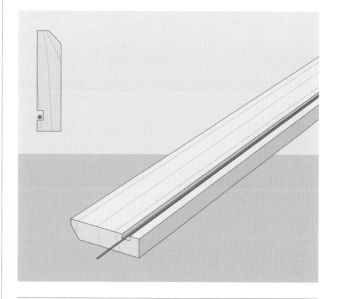

router, bit storage

When making raised panel doors for your kitchen (or other) cabinets you will invariably use several different types of router bits on your router table. Dropping any one of these expensive bits can make for a costly accident. Take a small piece of acrylic and drill a half dozen ½" holes in them. Screw the plastic to the top edge of your router table fence.

router, bit storage

Router bits should never be stored loose in a drawer or box; the bit's edges can easily chip, and a chipped carbide bit can be dangerous to use. I built a mobile router table and I like to keep the bits handy with a simple storage panel made from ¾" plywood. You can mount it on your router table base or drill some through holes to hang it from pegboard.

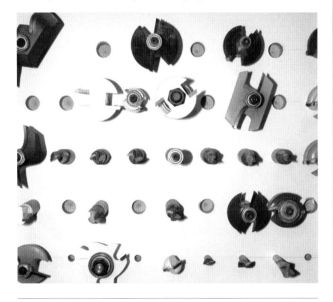

router, compass

Making a shop-built trammel or router compass will allow you to route small or large circles. Use your existing router base as a pattern. The pivot slot should be centered on the trammel. You can make from either ¼" Plexiglas or Masonite.

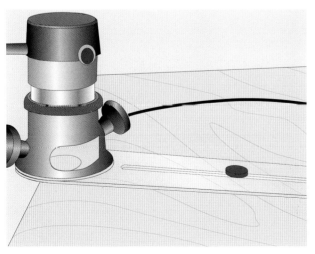

router, boring long holes

Boring long holes in a lamp base for the wire can sometimes be a daunting task. However, that hole can be made beforehand with a router. Before turning on the lathe, select your piece of wood and rip it down the center. Lay the two pieces flat and rout a groove down the center of each piece. Be sure to stop an inch or so from either end to give your lathe spurs something to grasp on to. Glue the two pieces back together and start turning.

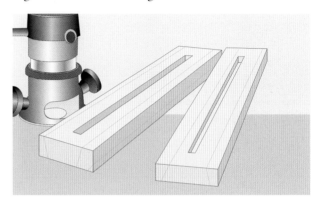

router, cutting radius

Measure the distance from the center of your router collet to the edge of the base plate. Write this dimension on the upper portion of the base for future reference when routing dadoes and other router work.

router, drawer grooves

Use your router table to route drawer bottom grooves for installing plywood drawer bottoms. Of course the drawers are not finished when you are doing this so you must either tape or use a web clamp to hold the drawer edges together. Use a guide bearing equipped slot router bit and carefully route the inside of the drawer sides. Square up the edges of the grooves with a chisel after removing the tape or the web clamp.

router, maintenance

Maintaining your plunge router is important as the plunge mechanism (rods) may stick at a crucial time. There is some debate over what kind of lubricant to use but I can say this, NEVER use oil! Oil or grease attracts dust and will defeat the original purpose of making the rods slick. Use silicone spray. The silicone is slick and doesn't attract dust or dirt. Powered graphite will also work. Dust some on the rods, then rub the graphite on the rods using a piece of newspaper. Run the plunge base up and down the rods a few times to work in the graphite. Lightly brush away the excess graphite dust and you're good to go.

router, flush cutting

Flush cutting plugs usually means some damage to the workpiece itself. To save this from happening, get out your router. Set the bottom-cutting bit just a hair above the surface of the workpiece. Put the router over and to one side of the plug and turn it on. A little sanding and the plug is gone.

router, moulding jig

A router table is not required if you make a straight-edge T-shaped jig out of ¾" plywood. Clamp the jig to a fairly wide board, route the moulding edge, and rip the piece to the desired width on your table saw.

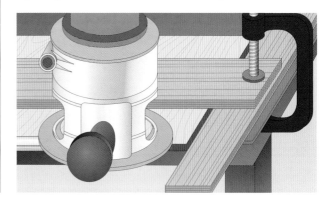

ROUTERS

The router is one of the most frequently used and versatile tools in any workshop. It can make mouldings, fancy edges, dadoes and cut circles and lettering. Many books have been written on this versatile tool, most notably *The New Router Handbook* by the late Patrick Spielman. The router can be used freehand or mounted upside down in a router table to give the tool even more versatility. The table-mounted router can be used as a shaper to make custom mouldings, raised panels and the stiles and rails that go with them. There are a variety of accessories available for the router that will further increase its versatility. The more versatile routers are available with a fixed base and a plunge base.

router, making mouldings

Making narrow mouldings with a router using wood strips is not a safe operation. The safest way of making these mouldings is to shape them on a wide board. Route one edge, flip the board and route the other edge. Use your table saw to cut the mouldings from the wider board.

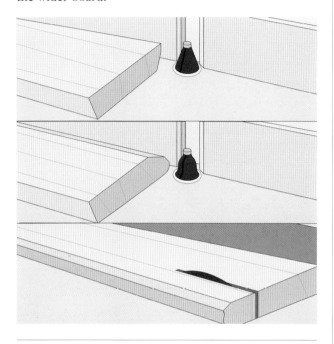

router, right hand rule

To take the rotation confusion out of the router it may be easier to remember the "Right Hand Rule". When facing the router close your hand but point straight ahead with the index finger. The curled thumb indicates the rotation of the router bit and the pointed finger indicates the direction in which to do your routing. Simple, eh?

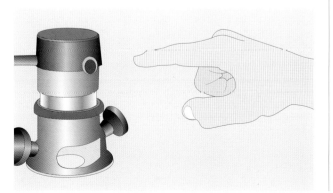

router, plunge adjustment

Should you be having a problem making a very fine adjustment with your plunge router try this simple solution. Place a sheet or two (or more) of paper under the edge of the router base and then plunge the bit.

router, small profiles

Putting a round-over or other shapes on narrow pieces of wood can be a dangerous operation on the router table. The opening on the table is usually too large to perform this safely; the router bit may dangerously grab the piece and perhaps your fingers. A zero-clearance router fence is the answer. Clamp a strip of Masonite hardboard to your router fence and turn on the router. The router bit will cut into the Masonite providing a smooth flush surface to rout those small end pieces.

router, stable base

To give your router base more stability while cutting a groove on a drawer box (the groove will accept a runner mounted in the cabinet), clamp a scrap strip of wood to the side. This strip will, of course, need to be flush with the surface you're routing.

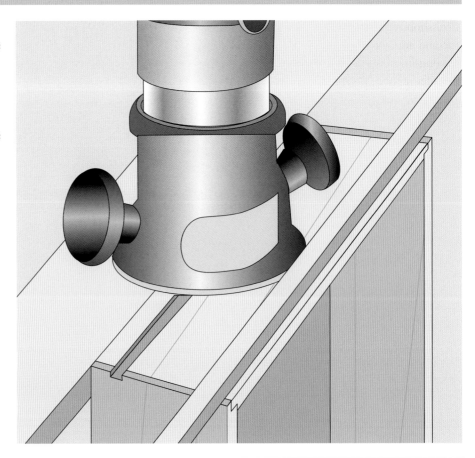

router, tables

Routers are made more versatile when they are mounted under a router table. Router tables of many types are available for sale as complete units, or you can buy the principal parts separately such as the tabletop or a fence unit. Some woodworkers prefer to make their own router tables, and these components make the work easier. There are many sources of plans for building your own router table on the internet.

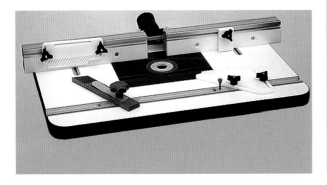

router, testing bits

Many router bits will produce different shapes just by raising or lowering them. Before determining the edge pattern, test your router bit on a scrap piece first to determine if that is the pattern you are looking for.

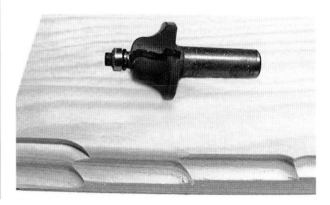

rulers

Steel shop rulers are always quite slippery on the back side and are sometimes difficult to hold secure while drawing lines. Apply double faced tape to the back of the ruler and then apply thin rubber sheeting or felt

sander, disc removing

Those pressure adhesive-backed (PSA) sanding discs go on the sander plate easily but can be tough to remove. No matter how careful you are, they always seem to tear and leave little bits stuck to the surface. Next time you have to replace one of these sanding discs, turn your machine on and sand a couple of scraps of wood. This will heat up the disc. Turn off the machine and unplug it. Now, peel off the disc. You will find it a much easier and neater task when the adhesive is warmed up. Another way to warm up the adhesive is to use a heat gun. Before placing a new disc on the wheel, use a little solvent to clean the wheel first. Make sure that the wheel is metal and not a plastic substance — the solvent may eat or melt the plastic.

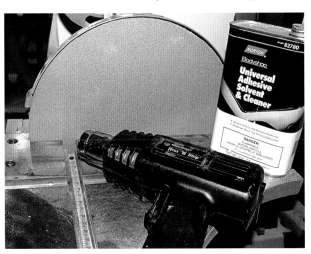

sander, disc perforating

Perforated sanding discs are more expensive than the plain ones. You can do your own perforations. A template using an existing perforated sanding disc laid on top of a plain disc can be used as a guide. Use a paper hole punch, steel punch or drill press to make the duplicate holes.

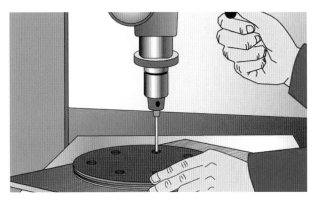

sander, disc storage

Sanding disc storage on dowels is a great way to keep the discs organized and ready to use. Label each disc as to its grit. It's also easy to see when you need more of a certain disc.

sander, disc storage

Should the dowels mentioned above get too full, the discs will have a tendency to creep forward and then fall off. To fix this, drill a small hole through the end of the dowel and insert a hitch pin, cotter pin or even a paper clip to hold the discs on.

sandpaper, cutting jig

With these jigs, you will save a lot of time cutting sandpaper. To make them, cut a piece of hardwood or plywood to the exact size of your ⅓- or ½-sheet orbital sander. Miter the long side. Drill a hole at the top center for pegboard hanging, and you now have a jig for cutting sandpaper to fit your sander.

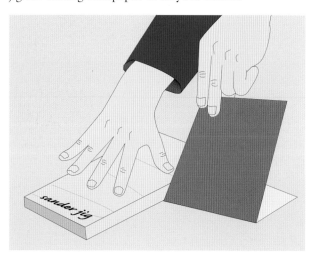

sander, disc storage

Another way of storing 5" sanding discs is to use CD-ROM plastic storage boxes. These file boxes usually come complete with index tabs. You can fit several hundred sanding discs in one box and you can mark the index tabs with the grit numbers.

sander pads, replacing

The pads on sanders that accept sticky-back sanding sheets can eventually get gummed up and will no longer accept the sandpaper. Find an old mouse pad, cut it to fit your sander and attach it using rubber cement.

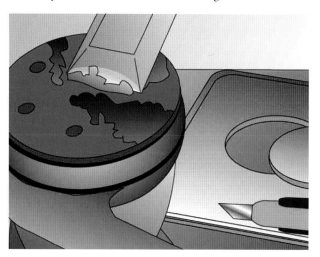

RANDOM ORBIT SANDERS

Random-orbital sanders (ROS) are probably the best power sanders to have come along since the invention of sandpaper. Random orbital sanders vary the pattern of their sanding in random circular motions and, therefore, the user is not restricted to sanding wood with the grain. Very seldom are swirls detected as sometimes occurs in orbital in-line sanders. Most random orbital sanders are of the "palm" type and these are usually 5"-diameter pad types. Some use sanding discs that have holes in them to facilitate the exhaust of sawdust through the sander itself. The sawdust is collected in a built-in receptacle or through the attachment of a shop vacuum.

sander pads, replacing

Should the old pad need removing this can be done very carefully with a utility knife and/or an adhesive solvent.

sander pads, replacing

The hook portion of the hook and loop pad on sanders often wears out and becomes ineffective. Replacement pads are available from Norton Abrasives that are self-adhesive backed and simply stick on to the existing worn out pad. You may have to make holes in them to match the old ones.

sanding blocks

There are probably hundreds of ways of making a shop-built sanding block and here is just one more that happens to be a favorite of mine. The wedge really secures the sandpaper tightly. As an option you may want to add a scrap of carpet underlay to soften the bottom surface.

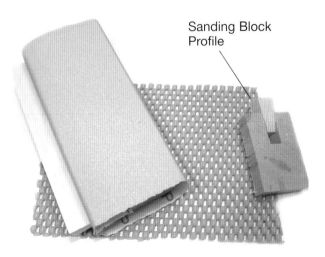

Sanding Block Profile

sanding discs, maintaining

Most woodworkers use crepe rubber blocks to clean sanding belts and drums to extend their life. These same crepe rubber blocks can also be used on sanding discs. Apply the block to the moving sanding disc or belt to more than double the abrasive life.

sandpaper belts, cleaning

If your sanding belts look like they are on their last legs, there might still be some life left in them. Use a brass brush with some oven cleaner to remove the tar and resin that builds up on the belts. The oven cleaner will not harm the abrasive or the adhesive.

sandpaper, alternates

There are sanding situations when you have to get in really tight and close. For just such occasions I raid my wife's manicure set and 'borrow' some emery boards. They do not wear as well as some of the more costly abrasive types, but they work well in a pinch.

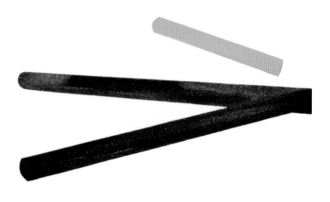

sandpaper belts, maintaining

Remember to release the pressure on the belts when you have finished using the belt sander. If you leave the pressure on them, they will soon stretch to their maximum and will cause both tracking problems and reduced tension at the platen. With sandpaper drum tubes, it is best to loosen up the nut that compresses the rubber drum after each use. The heat buildup created by the spinning tube will bond it to the rubber drum and make removal difficult.

Loosen

Undo Nut

sandpaper, belt storage

Sandpaper belts and drum tubes need to be stored properly. Throwing them into a drawer or bin may crack the adhesive holding the grit and will shorten their lives. I cut some dowels (broom handles will do as well) and screw them through the back of pegboard. The belts can be inter-stacked to save space; the tubes require more lengthy dowels. Keep the belts arranged by grit and length.

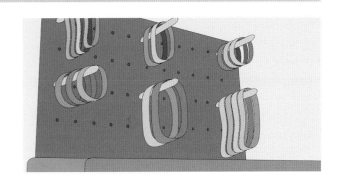

sandpaper, roll cutting

Cutting a straight edge on sandpaper from rolls is best done using the back of a rip or crosscut hand saw.

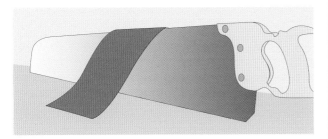

sandpaper, sheet storing

Sandpaper sheets have a tendency to curl when left on a shelf or in a drawer. To properly store sandpaper, remove any wrapping of paper or plastic. The best way to store all sandpaper, is to lay it flat, abrasive side down, on a shelf or in a drawer with a weight on it. Sanding belts or drums should be stored either on edge or hanging from a dowel.

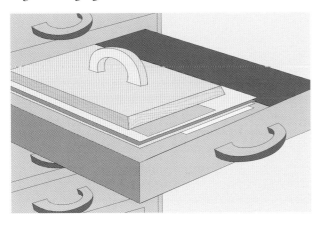

sandpaper, roll storage

Storing rolls of sandpaper is easy if you use lengths of ABS plastic pipe. Cut 2½" diameter pipe in 3" lengths. Use your band saw to make a cut on the length of the pipe. Screw the pipe lengths to a piece of ¾" plywood and hang it handy to the rest of your abrasives. Insert the roll of sandpaper in the tube and feed an end through the slot. The edge will also act as a cutter.

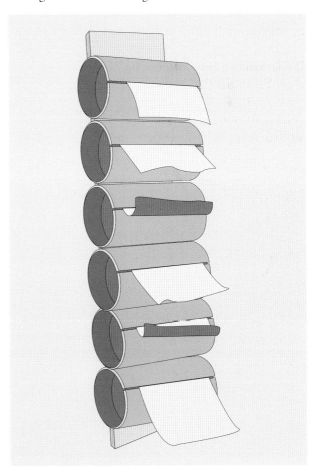

sandpaper, sheet cutting

Cutting sandpaper to size is easily done with this sandpaper jig. Cut a piece of ¾" scrap plywood 12" × 15", screw a 10" hacksaw blade to the plywood and mark it for ¼, ⅓ and ½ sheet cuts. Place a couple of thin washers between the saw blade and the plywood.

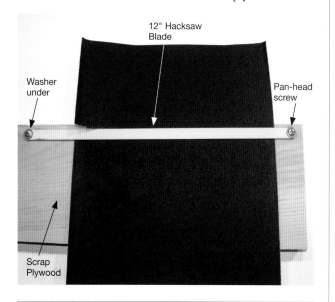

12" Hacksaw Blade

Washer under

Pan-head screw

Scrap Plywood

sandpaper, types/application

In addition to the various grit numbers on sandpaper, there are a number of different sandpaper types, as previously mentioned. A general rule of thumb for the various grit types and their common applications is shown in the following chart:

Grit Type	Application
Aluminum Oxide	Softwoods & Hardwoods
Emery Paper or Cloth	Between finish coats or on soft metals (copper or aluminum).
Flint Paper	Softwoods
Garnet Paper	Softwoods & Medium hardwoods

sandpaper, used application

Don't throw away those used sandpaper sheets, pads or discs; save them, as they can be used for hand-sanding jobs. After they have been used on power sanders, they become more pliable and can be used in tight corners and for lathe work.

sawdust, static

Static can build up in sawdust collection systems that use PVC (polyvinyl chloride), ABS or metal pipes. Although there have not been many reports of explosions due to this, you can get quite a shock if you touch the pipe. To avoid this, wrap some copper wire around a section of it and connect the wire to the ground on an electrical outlet.

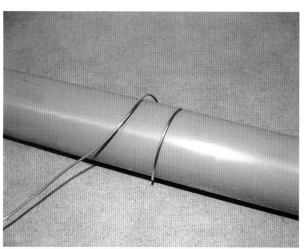

sawdust, static

Most safety glasses are made of plastic; and plastic attracts sawdust. Many times I have put on a safety shield covered in sawdust, only to think that maybe somebody turned off the lights. To help minimize sawdust buildup on your safety glasses, wipe them occasionally with a used sheet of fabric softener. It will stop static cling.

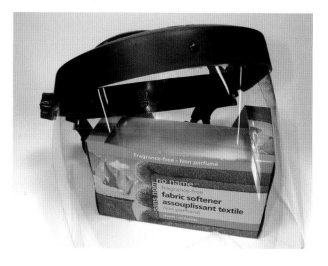

scrapers, making

There is no need to run down to your woodworking supply store for a scraper. Check your saw collection: I'll bet you'll find one you haven't used in years. Select the one with the thinnest gauge steel. Use a felt pen to mark out the shape you want and then use a jig saw with a metal-cutting blade or a Dremel tool to cut out the pattern. Be sure that the back of the saw blade becomes the edge of your scraper (it's truer). The Dremel tool can be used to de-burr the edges and do the final shaping.

screwdriver, magnetizing

Screws won't stay on the tips of most screwdrivers except perhaps Roberston (square drive) screws. There are times when you wish you had three hands when placing screws in tight places. Here's help. Place a small rare earth magnet on the screwdriver just above the blade. By doing this even a slot type screw will stay in place.

Rare Earth Magnet

scraper handle, making

A scraper can be made easier to use if it has a handle. Use a scrap piece of ¾" stock 2" longer and 1" narrower than the scraper you are using. Sand and finish the wood block. Drill holes in the ends of the scraper and use pan-head screws and washers to fasten it to the wood. Drill a hole to facilitate a T-nut and thumb screw. The thumb screw will bow the scraper as required.

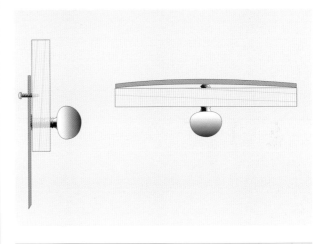

screwdriver, re-using

Never throw old screwdrivers away unless they are really bent out of shape. They can be re-ground to become a very useful tool. For example, grinding them to a point will turn them into a useful scratch awl. Grinding an old flat-headed screwdriver to give it a razor-sharp blade will turn it into a chisel. Cut a thin V-slot in the blade and then bend it. You now have a brad or staple remover. Other uses include a punch, a nail set, etc.

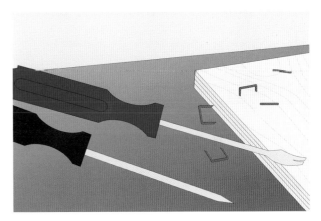

screws, cordless drill holder

Ryobi did it first when they put a magnetic surface on the base of their cordless drill/drivers. These are handy for holding screws and other items that you may be needing. Use epoxy to adhere a rare earth magnet to your cordless drill for the same purpose.

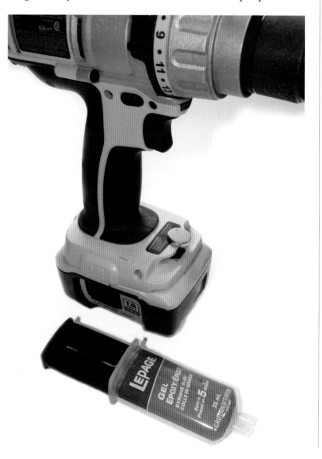

screws, pocket-hole jig

Pocket holes are an exceptionally good way to join cabinetry components because the screws are completely hidden. Commercially made pocket hole jigs can be expensive. Here's a way to get professional-looking pocket holes with a simple shop-made jig. Use a 1" × 1" piece of maple or similar hardwood and cut it to a 3" length. The usual angle for pocket holes is 15 degrees, so cut one inch off the maple at a 15 degree angle. Rotate the pieces and glue them back together as shown here. Using a ⅜" drill bit, drill a hole all the way through the center of the longer piece. That's the jig. To use it, simply clamp it to your workpiece and use the same ⅜" drill bit to drill a shallow hole into your workpiece. A smaller drill bit is used to counterbore. Some testing on a scrap piece may be required to get it just right.

scroll saw, extending blade usage

Most scroll-saw users use thin wood for their intricate scroll-work. Doing so will wear out the bottom portion of the saw blades, leaving the top portion virtually unused. There is a way to use this unused area that will not compromise your work. A supplemental table made of ¾" plywood or MDF can be cut to fit the top of your existing saw table, and, when affixed to the table with double-faced tape, will make use of the still-sharp scroll-saw blade area.

scroll saw, patterns

When making an intricately scrolled cut as a repeat pattern on your scroll saw you only need to cut half of the pattern. Lay it down on your workpiece, draw the pattern, flip it over and draw that half.

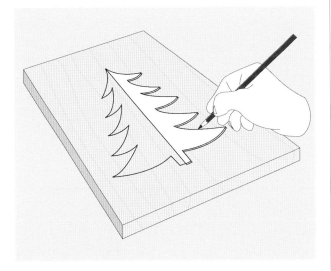

scroll saw, storing blades

Keeping your scroll-saw blades together when you are working on an intricate workpiece is made easier with a rare earth magnet or two. Simply place the magnets on a non-moving part at the rear of the machine.

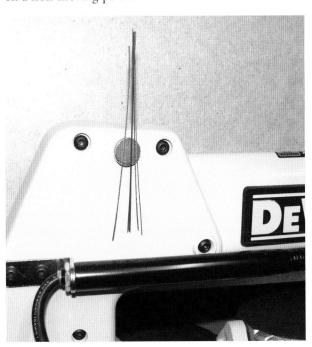

scroll saw, storing blades

Scroll-saw blades are easily lost in tool drawers because they are so thin. A good way of keeping track of them is to store them in plastic tubes or cigar tubes. Use masking tape to mark the type of blade inside.

scroll saw, thin blades

Can't quite grasp that extra fine scroll saw blade for installing it. Here's the tried and true method. Use a small spring clamp to hold it in position while you clamp it in the saw.

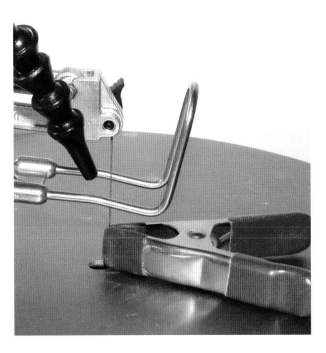

scroll saw, thin material

Using your scroll saw to cut thin materials can prove to be a difficult task. The thin material has a tendency to ride with the blade and do a lot of flapping. Double-faced tape to the rescue! Tape your thin material to a thicker piece of scrap material, being sure to keep the tape away from the cutting area. Doing this will have an added benefit; it will become a template for future work. Also, do not remove the scrap piece until you've done some edge-sanding. The scrap will make this job easier as well.

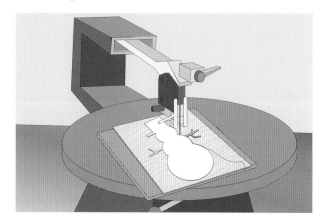

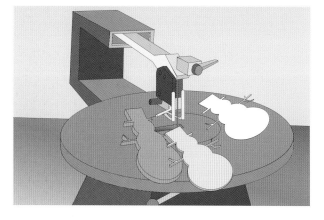

shaper head

A shaper head (also known as a moulding head) is a heavy steel disc into which variously shaped blades or knives are fitted. It is used on a table saw or radial arm saw. The most common use of the shaper head is for making long lengths of mouldings such as baseboard and window or door trim or for furniture. The most commonly used is the one from Sears Craftsman, and they have about 24 different knife sets for the tool. The shaper head is installed on the arbor of your table saw or radial arm saw and the head is designed to take off a little at a time, so several passes will need to be made. Shaping is usually done running with the wood grain. To vary the shape of the moulding, move your saw fence and install a different set of knives.

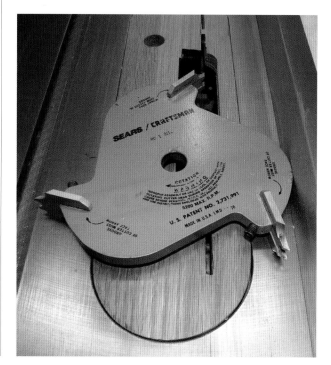

shaper head, crosscutting

You can use a shaper head in crosscutting operations. Some of these may include making dadoes for shelves or for rabbet joints. The problem that occurs is "tear-out" at the end of the cut. To avoid this, you can take one of two precautionary steps. One, if your finished piece is to be 12" wide, make it 13" before using the shaper head and then trim it down to cut out the tear-out area. Two, place a piece of wood scrap at the exiting edge of your workpiece.

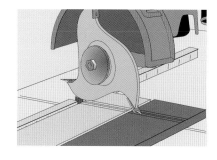

shaper inserts, sharpening

Don't let the complex shapes of shaper inserts confound you. Generally, it is only the edge that needs honing, and this can be done on an oilstone. Oil the stone liberally and hone only the flat side. Be sure, however, that the stone is perfectly flat. Check it out with a straightedge.

socket wrenches

Some socket-wrench sets are sold in rather flimsy plastic-molded containers that can fall apart pretty quickly. To make these containers more rigid and retain their shapes, spray the backs of them with a can of low-expansion spray-foam insulation. While the insulation is still expanding, place the plastic back into the original box and place the sockets in it. The foam will harden and hold those sockets for quite some time.

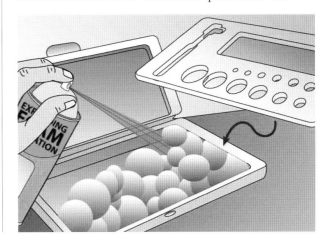

steel square, making square

The steel square or builder's square is an invaluable tool in any workshop. Usually, the body, as the long side is called, is 24" long and the tongue is either 12" or 16" long. These measurements conform to the standard stud and joist placements. The body is generally 2" wide and the tongue 1½" wide. The outside corner is called the heel. A *framing* square differs from a steel square in that it has a number of scales printed or etched on the body, the tongue or both. These scales usually consist of a scale which tells how long a 45-degree brace should be to support a given shelf size, a board measurement scale, an angle-cutting scale and a rafter scale. If, after testing your steel square, you find that it is not true, there are a number of options, the last of which is to junk it. First, though, try this technique: After checking the square and determining that it is out of square on the high side (for example, 90.5, 91, or 92 degrees), draw a straight line from the heel to the inside corner of the square. With a pointed punch and a heavy steel mallet, hit a spot on the line close to the heel. Check the square

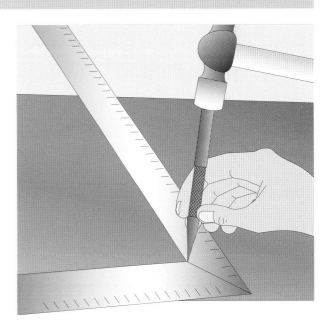

for accuracy. Hit it again in the same spot if it needs it. Conversely, if the out-of-square is on the low side (for example, 89.5, 89, or 88 degrees), do the same as above, but use the punch close to the inside comer.

171

straight edge, bargain price

You can buy an 8'-long straightedge for just a few bucks and very little work. These are called metal wall studs and building supply stores have them readily available.

table saw, accurate angles

When crosscutting angles on your table saw, you want to be absolutely certain of their accuracy. A protractor will help you attain this. Set the protractor to 45 degrees. Place it against the miter gauge and the saw blade. Adjust and lock the miter gauge. Use an awl to scribe a line across the saw table. Now you have a permanent reference line for future alignment.

straight edge, makeshift

Don't have a straight edge handy? Need one quickly? For short lines up to 18" or so, simply flip your tape measure over.

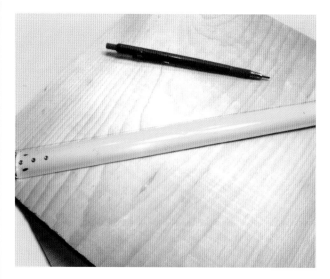

table saw, accuracy

Should you be having trouble getting precise 45-degree bevel miter cuts on your table saw, the problem may not be with the saw. Try cleaning the bevel stop with an air gun. The problem probably lies with sawdust building up on the stop.

TABLE SAWS

What is a workshop without a table saw? Every shop has one in some form or other. They can be stationary floor-model tools or bench-top tools. There are combination tools like the ShopSmith that adapt to a table saw. Some woodworkers prefer using a radial arm saw as the basic wood-cutting tool. Whichever tool you have, the most important thing to remember is to routinely check the components of the saw for proper function and accuracy. The tilting arbor on the table saw must be accurate to provide precise bevel-cutting. This should be checked at both the 45 and 90 degree positions.

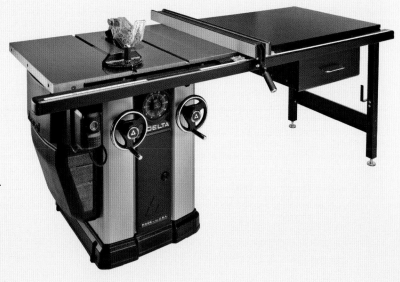

table saw, bowed wood

Cutting bowed wood on your table saw is unsafe. Straighten the boards by using a J-channel; the type used for vinyl siding. Boards up to 1" thick will fit nicely into the channel. Use double-faced tape to secure the board to the channel.

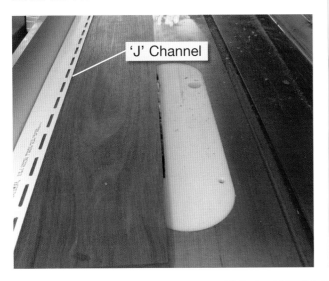

'J' Channel

table saw, butterflies

Butterflies used to reinforce edge-joined boards are easily made on the table saw using a length of hardwood. It is important the grain runs the length of the butterfly for strength. The table saw blade is set at 10 degrees and raised to half the height of the required butterfly. Set your rip fence to the proper width and then make four cuts.

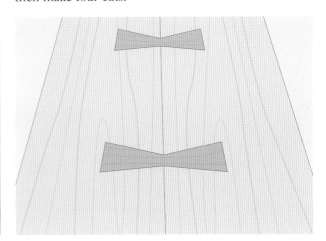

table saw, changing blade

Changing saw blades on a table saw can be risky; the teeth are sharp and can cause severe injury. Here's a safe way of doing it: Cut a piece of 2×4 about 12" long. Place the board on your table saw directly over the completely-lowered blade. The top center of the blade should be midway on the length of the board. Set your fence for a ¾" cut. Clamp the 2×4 securely to the fence, turn on the saw and slowly raise the blade into the 2×4. Raise the blade to a height of 2½". Lower the saw blade and turn off the saw. The result will be a slot in the 2×4 that can be used to brace the fully-raised saw blade when you are removing or installing it. Keep the 2×4 for future use when you change your table-saw blades.

173

table saw, changing blade

To safely (for your hands and the blade teeth) remove a table-saw blade from the arbor, use a crepe block. These are the blocks that are used to clean sanding belts. Wedge the crepe between the table and the blade and loosen the arbor nut with a wrench. The crepe block can also be used to help install a new blade on the saw.

table saw, cross cuts

To make repeat crosscuts on the table saw, screw a long auxiliary hardwood face to your table-saw miter gauge. Clamp or screw a stop block to it.

table saw, changing blade

When changing blades on your table saw, invariably the arbor washer will end up in a pile of sawdust inside the tool. I purchased a gooseneck-style of LED flashlight with a rare earth magnet on the end. The magnet will find it but the light adds a little more assurance. It works like a charm and sometimes it finds other small parts that have inadvertently fallen into those sawdust depths.

table saw, dado blades

When using a dado blade set or a dado wobble blade in your table saw, be sure to use an auxiliary fence attached to your saw's rip fence. This allows you to rabbets without damaging your blades or fence.

table saw, dust collection

Mounting a piece of ½" plywood or MDF (medium density fiberboard) between your contractor- type saw and the steel base will help with sawdust collection. Drill a hole in the board and install a 4" plumbing flange. The opening should hold a standard 4" dust-collection hose.

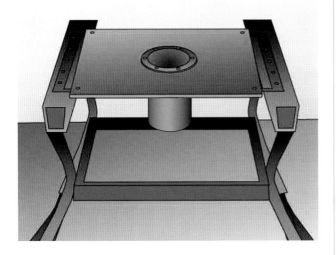

table saw, fence

Some woodworkers don't like the finish on their table-saw's rip fence. To counter this they have removed them and installed standard wide aluminum extrusions that will accept T-bolts. Mount the extrusion using T-bolts inserted though holes drilled through the fence — tighten with washers and wing nuts. The new fence extrusion can be used on either side of the fence and it can be longer if desired. It can also be pulled back towards the back of the saw for crosscutting operations. Note: The applicable extrusion may be available through your tool retailer or through www.8020.net. The pictured profile is called no. 3034–lite.

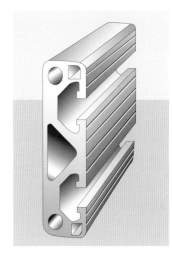

table saw, fence safety

Never use your rip fence on your table saw as a stop when using your miter gauge. Doing so will inevitably jam the piece between the fence and the blade and kick it back at you causing serious injury. Use an auxiliary fence clamped to your rip fence ONLY at the very front of your rip fence.

table saw, fence storage

Safely store your rip fence for your table saw when it is not in use. Use a length of white 6" ABS drain pipe. Screw it to the side of the base of your saw or to the legs of the extension table. I drilled a couple of holes in mine and used nylon tie wraps to secure it.

table saw, link belts

The regular V-belts that drive your saw's arbor can sometimes cause vibration. Although this does not usually impair the accuracy of the saw, the constant vibration can put stress on both the arbor and the tilt mechanism. Link belts are made from a heavy-duty material and are infinitely adjustable by simply removing or adding a link. The main advantage of using them is that they are virtually vibration-free and will greatly extend the life of your saw.

table saw, miter gauge adj.

A second method uses a builder's square. Set the miter gauge in the left table-saw slot and your builder's square long side in the right-hand slot. Use the tail of the square to true-up the gauge.

table saw, miter gauge adj.

You can't get square crosscuts on a table saw if your miter gauge is out of whack! To quickly set it back to square, turn the gauge upside down and slide it into the saw's miter slot. Where the edge of the gauge meets the table-saw edge, it should sit flush. If you see any light between the two edges, it's time to adjust the miter gauge. Loosen the gauge handle, fit the gauge tight against the saw table, and tighten the handle. Flip the miter gauge over and adjust the pointer accordingly.

table saw, miter gauge adj.

You may have noticed that the slots on your table saw or band saw are a little lower than the thickness of the bar. When the miter gauge is used with larger pieces of wood the gauge can catch on the edge of the saw's table. Preventing this is easy: Grind or file a 45-degree angle on the edge of the saw's table.

table saw, miter gauge fix

As miter gauges are used, they may tend to get sloppy in the tracks and therefore lose their accuracy. One way to correct this is to peen the edges of the gauge's guide bar with a pointed steel punch. This puts small dimples in the bar. At least four dimples should be made, two in front and two at the back of the gauge. Hammer the punch lightly at first to determine the feel or tightness of the bar.

table saw, miter gauge fix

The miter-gauge slots on table saws and other power tools are machined very precisely and the edges can be quite sharp to the touch. Take a moment to use a file or some emery cloth to remove the sharpness. You'll be glad you did.

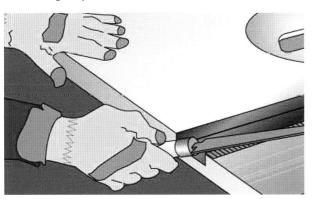

table saw, miter gauge fix

Another method of removing play in the miter gauge is to use strips of aluminum duct-sealing tape. Run a strip down both edges of the miter gauge bar. Add more if required.

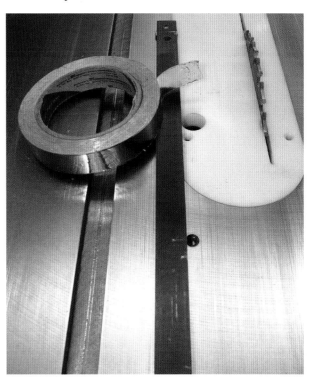

table saw, mobile base

Commercial mobile bases for your stationary tools can be fairly expensive, but, if you have some scrap hardwood lying around you can make your own. You can buy locking casters but this brake is a sure fire way to keep the tools secure. The brake board is flush with the floor. Bear in mind that you'll to compensate for the slightly rising base.

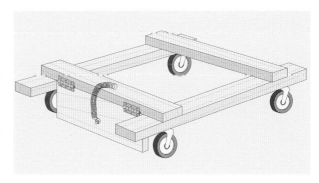

table saw, outfeed roller

The shop-made outfeed table-saw roller shown here was built from hardwood scrap pieces. The center post rides in a sleeve and is tightened in position with a hex bolt and T-nut. The roller is from an old typewriter (remember those?). The base on mine was made from an old store display stand, but you can use plywood in a similar fashion. The post will elevate high enough to work with my band saw and low enough for my thickness planer. I made reference marks on the post for the various tools to make adjusting quicker. Because it is a single roller, it is important that it be parallel and level to the tool to prevent pulling to one side.

table saw, panel doors

Don't have a style-and-rail router bit set? Fear not! I can help you make stile-and-rail panel doors without it. Use your table saw to cut the groove in the stiles and rails. To perfectly center the groove, run it through the saw, flip it over and run it through again. This may require using some scrap pieces to get the exact width required.

table saw, outfeed table

In a pinch, you might look in the laundry room for a temporary out-feed table. An ironing board will do, and they can usually be adjusted to any height. Check with your spouse first and make sure you remove the ironing pad before using it.

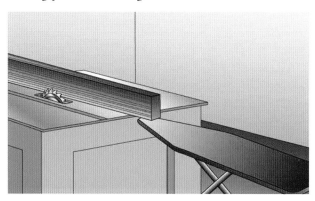

table saw, ripping dowels

Cutting a groove into the length of a dowel or other long round workpiece is made easier and safer if you cut two squares from scrap that are the same dimension as the diameter of the dowel. Glue (with hot melt glue) these to the ends of the dowel and run it through the table saw. Use the same method to flatten one side of a round workpiece.

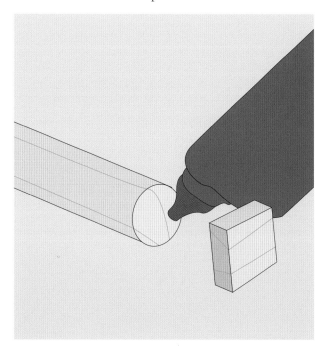

table saw, stops

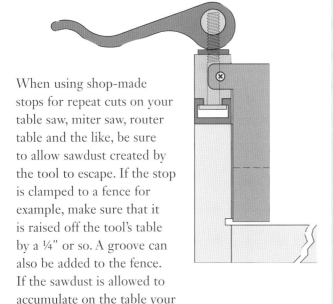

When using shop-made stops for repeat cuts on your table saw, miter saw, router table and the like, be sure to allow sawdust created by the tool to escape. If the stop is clamped to a fence for example, make sure that it is raised off the tool's table by a ¼" or so. A groove can also be added to the fence. If the sawdust is allowed to accumulate on the table your work will be inaccurate.

table saw, top (polishing)

Buffing up the wax that you have just applied to your cast-iron machine table tops is easier and more efficient with felt pads or a lamb's wool bonnet attached to your random-orbital sander. If you have the hook-and-loop pad, place a piece of 80-grit sandpaper on one the sander first. This will prevent the "fuzz" of the felt from clogging the pad. Felt may be purchased at fabric stores.

table saw, table maintenance

A clean saw table will produce easier and more accurate cuts. Steel tabletops are susceptible to rust and, as a result, pitting and even warping. To prevent this from happening, a good table maintenance program is in order. Every six months or so, use paint thinner or even WD40 oil and very fine steel wool to clean the top surface. Wipe the surface clean and then generously apply a coat of Rust Check and let it sit overnight. Wipe it all off and then apply a coat of paste wax and buff it to a shine.

table saw, throat plate

There is a quicker and easier way to adjust shop-made throat plates for your table saw. Instead of trying to use shims to bring the plate flush with the table saw's top surface, try using a few dabs of hot melt glue. The glue will stick to the throat plate but not the cast iron on the table.

table saw, zero clearance

A zero-clearance table-saw "insert" helps reduce tear-out and deflects a lot of sawdust from the material you are cutting. Shown here is a temporary one made for the table saw. It is a piece of plywood attached to the saw's tabletop. Lower the saw blade, adjust the fence and use double-faced tape to hold the plywood in place. Now turn your saw on. Slowly raise the blade to the desired height (a little more than the thickness of the workpiece you're cutting.)

tape measure, accuracy

Tape measures can vary in accuracy by as much as a ½" in 8' from one manufacturer to another. It is important to use the same manufacturer's tape measure when transferring dimensions.

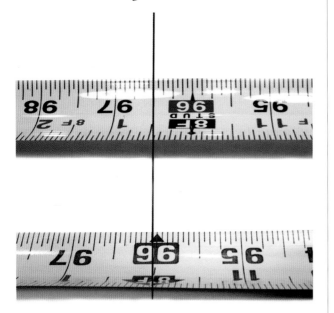

table saw, zero clearance

A zero-clearance table-saw insert can be made from hardwood or plywood. Trace your metal insert on the wood and cut it out. Drill a finger hole to make it easier to remove. Once you have cut it to shape, lower your table-saw blade below the table surface, position the insert into the opening and turn on the saw.

Holding the insert in position with a push stick, slowly raise the saw blade to cut through the insert. When finished, turn off the saw and remove the insert. Use a permanent marker to indicate the type of saw blade that you used. A separate insert may be required for specific types of blades.

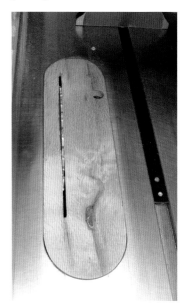

tape measure, compass

Most tape measures have a slot on the tang or hook end; this slot allows a common nail head to fit into it. If you want to draw a circle for a pattern, drive a common nail into the center of the proposed circle. Hook the slot of the tape measure tang on the nail head, set the tape measure to the correct radius, and hold a pencil against the body of it. Make sure you compensate for the pencil thickness and the offset of the nail head.

Common Nail Head

tape measure, inside measurements

I have a problem when it comes to making precise inside measurements with a tape measure. Most tape measures have "add 3 inches" printed on the case, some use 2½" and some others have a small window on the top. When I look down on the tape measure, either the window always seems to be dirty or scratched or the cases seem to protrude to make accuracy difficult. I've found a solution that works. I lay a combination square inside the area to be measured. I know that the square's blade is exactly 12" long. I measure up to the blade and add the 12". It works every time.

tape measure, scribing

The tape measure is not just used for measuring, it can also be used as a scribing tool. Assuming you want to scribe a line parallel to the edge of a sheet or piece of plywood, simply grasp the tape at your measurement and use the hook to scribe your line. There is also a tape measure available that has a built-in carbon marker that will scribe a line for those that do a lot of scribing.

tape measure, stick-on

Sticky-backed tape measures work well on your radial arm saw or compound miter saw. Stick a strip an inch or two above the table, on the fence. They are available to read in both directions.

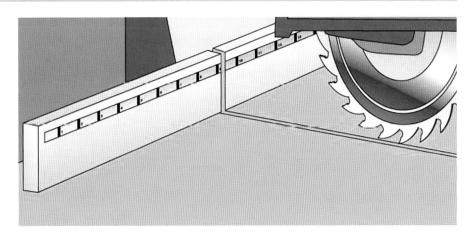

thickness planer, knife fix

Once in a while the inevitable happens and you hit a piece of metal that leaves a small nick in your thickness-planer blades. Every piece of wood that you plane after that will have a small raised stripe on it. Don't fret; there is a quick fix. You don't have to dismantle the entire tool and have all of the knives resharpened just yet. With the power cord unplugged, open the knife access panel and loosen one knife only. Slide the knife just slightly to the left or right and then reinstall it. This will alter the track and the one knife will erase that raised area.

thickness planer, snipe

To eliminate snipe on your thickness planer, feed a similar scrap board with the same thickness directly behind your workpiece. Or, place two narrow, longer pieces on either side of the workpiece. The scrap pieces will get sniped instead of the workpiece. Or, you can feed a workpiece that is longer than required through the planer and then cut off the snipe, leaving you with the right length for your job.

thickness planer, small parts

Sometimes workpieces are just too small to safely place in a thickness planer. Here is a safe way of handling them: Spot-glue or nail two long strips of wood of the same thickness as your workpiece to its sides to form an H. Slowly feed this H-shaped jig through the planer. When finished, remove the scraps.

toolkit

Those canvas inserts for plastic buckets are a great way to lug tools around. What they don't provide for, however, is a convenient place to keep an extension cord. Drill a hole near the bottom of the bucket for the cord. Coil the cord inside the bucket and feed the male (plug) end out of the hole. That can be fed to an outlet, and the remaining cord inside can be uncoiled for your power tools.

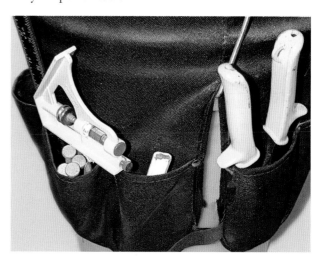

toothbrushes, in the shop

Don't throw away those old toothbrushes; keep a couple in your tool drawer. An old toothbrush can be used to clean pitch build-up on your blades and bits, clean files and rasps, clean small metal parts and, when stripping furniture, a toothbrush will get the stripper into intricate carving details.

utility knife, blade safety

Don't simply toss those used utility-knife and snap-off blades in the garbage. You may have to reach in there for something or someone else may have to. Get hold of a used prescription pill bottle, preferably a child-proof one. Cut a small slit in the top and when you are done with a sharp blade, insert it into the bottle. When the bottle is full, take it to your pharmacy. They have sources to safely dispose of sharpies.

vacuum, bench outlet

Using portable and bench-top tools close to or on your workbench usually means traipsing a shop vacuum hose with you — which may be both awkward and inconvenient. How about installing a vacuum outlet on the back surface of your workbench? It will be a lot more convenient.

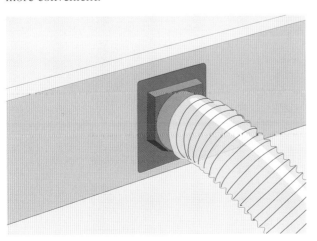

vacuum, more efficiency

To make your shop vacuum a little more efficient, use a pair of panty hose over the standard pleated filter. These will help keep the pleated filter clean and keep even more dust out of the shop.

vacuum, workshop

This technique of picking up nails with a vacuum is effective and saves me a lot of bending and stooping. I came up with the idea when I was tearing down walls to build my new workshop. I was trying to be economical by saving the 2×4s, so, needless to say, I had to remove the nails from them. Being lazy, I just let the nails drop on the floor, thinking I would sweep them up later. Well, a push broom doesn't work. All it does is make dust and hardly moves the nails. Then I had a brilliant idea. Using some epoxy glue, I glued a fairly strong magnet to the suction part of my vacuum cleaner. I positioned it about ½" above the bottom of the vacuum cleaner head so it would lift the nails off the floor and not jam them under the head. Now, I occasionally lift the wand, pluck off the nails and continue to vacuum.

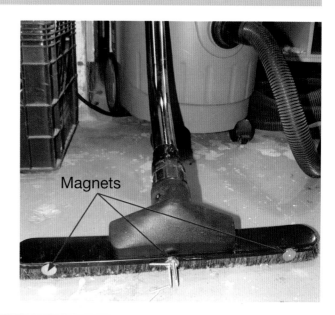

Magnets

veneer, applying

A quick-and-easy way to apply veneer to small, flat workpieces is to use adhesive fabric. This is available at most fabric shops. Lay it between the veneer and your stock, place a piece of brown paper on top, and use a hot, dry iron to press it all in place. Make sure that you get the iron to all of the edges.

Iron-On Adhesive Fabric

veneer, cutting

Wood veneer is much too thin to cut on a power saw, but sometimes this has to be done. Here is a shortcut: Sandwich the veneer between a couple of scrap pieces of ⅛" or ¼" plywood using double-faced tape to adhere them. Draw your pattern on the top surface and proceed to saw. Carefully separate the pieces when they are completed.

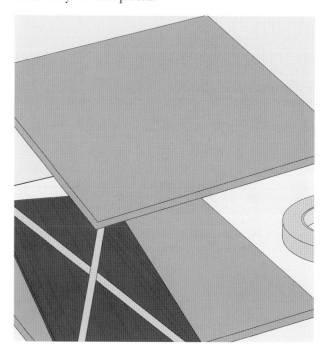

veneer, gluing

Gluing veneer is a slow process if you are gluing both sides of the workpiece, unless you have a commercial veneering press. You have to glue one side of the veneer and then one side of your workpiece, let them dry, and then repeat the process for the other side. This shortcut will expedite the gluing process: Apply contact cement to one side, then tap a 1" finishing nail into each corner of this side. Flip it over so that the board is resting on the nails and apply glue to this side. Apply glue to the veneer pieces. When they are tacky and ready to apply, adhere them to the top surface, flip it over, remove the nails and veneer that side.

Nails raise the workpiece

Apply glue on this side first

vise, vertical planing

The shop-made vertical-planing vise shown here is a great tool to have around the shop. It allows you to secure your workpiece so that you can work on its edge. The one that I have seen on various job sites is made primarily for the planing of door edges. I modified this one by making it a sliding jig. This allows you to clamp workpieces of varying thickness. The wing nuts and washers ensure that the workpiece is held firmly. Using two of these vises will keep your larger workpieces secure for planing or sanding.

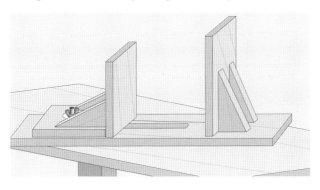

vise, determine diameter

Determining the diameter or thickness of a workpiece can be done even if you don't have calipers. Put the piece in either a bench vise or a bar clamp. Slightly tighten the vise or clamp and then measure the opening with a ruler or tape measure.

wire wheels, extending life

After a wire wheel has been used to remove rust or paint, the wires seem to all be running in the same direction and the wheel tends to lose its effectiveness. To extend the life of the wheel, after every use remove it from the arbor and reverse it. You'll probably double its life.

GRAHAM'S FINAL SHORTCUT

My mentors over the years have always told me to never take any wooden nickels. Never have, never will! Because, money doesn't grow on trees.

THE TOP SHOP USES FOR DUCT TAPE

Attach pieces of wood for full-size mockup.

Quick tie for extension cord.

Replace missing hinges.

Depth marker on drill bit.

Fix your safety glasses.

Pulling splinters.

Temporary clamp for gluing.

Replacement grip on tools or clamp handles.

Repair a broken pencil.

Straight line divider for painting or staining.

Closing the air gaps in the dust collector hose.

INDEX

MORE GREAT TITLES FROM POPULAR WOODWORKING!

MEASURE TWICE, CUT ONCE

By Jim Tolpin

From design and layout to developing a cutting list, Jim Tolpin's easy-to-follow style introduces a variety of tools (new and old) used to transfer measurements accurately to the wood. You'll learn the best cutting techniques, how to prevent mistakes before they happen, and for those unavoidable mistakes, you'll learn how to fix them so no one will know!

ISBN 13: 978-1-55870-809-9
ISBN 10: 1-55870-809-X
paperback, 128 p., #Z0835

ISBN 13: 978-1-55870-816-7
ISBN 10: 1-55870-816-2
paperback, 128 p., #Z0991

I CAN DO THAT! WOODWORKING PROJECTS

Edited by David Thiel

You can do that, quickly, easily and save money. Each project requires a minimum of tools, inexpensive materials found at your local home center. You'll also learn how to use each tool, which makes this book perfect for the beginning woodworker. The projects are fun and easy to make and are practical.

THE PERFECT EDGE

by Ron Hock

If you've never experienced the pleasure of using a really sharp, you're missing one of the real pleasures of woodworking. The mystery of the elusive sharp edge is solved. This book covers all the different sharpening methods so you can improve your sharpening techniques using your existing set-up or determine which one will best suet your needs and budget.

ISBN 13: 978-1-55870-858-7
ISBN 10: 1-55870-858-8,
hardcover, 224 p., #Z2676

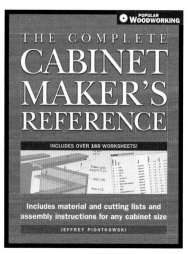

ISBN 13: 978-1-55870-757-3
ISBN 10: 1-55870-757-3
hardcover w/ concealed wire-o
256 p., #70710

THE COMPLETE CABINETMAKER'S REFERENCE

By Jeffrey Piontkowski

This indispensable resource for cabinetmakers includes cutting and assembly instructions, along with lists of types and quantities of materials needed for all standard-sized cabinets. You'll also learn how to adapt the projects to build custom-sized pieces.

These and other great woodworking books are available at your local bookstore, woodworking stores or from online suppliers.

www.popularwoodworking.com